VOCATIONAL ASTROLOGY

ILLUMINATING THE PATH TO CAREER SUCCESS

Viktor Simon

HU
HOUSE
PUBLISHING

HEARTS UNLEASHED HOUSE PUBLISHING

To contact the author please email him at:

Email: astrovicktor@gmail.com

www.astroviktor.com

Cover: Mayra Medina

Digital editing & coding: Oded Talmon

Charts: Solar Fire (Esoteric Technologies)

Layout: Viktor Simon

ISBN: 979-8-9882783-1-3

Summary

We spend 50% or more of our lives at work. 60-70% of people go to work simply to make money and do not truly enjoy what they do. In his work, author Viktor Simon, has helped thousands of people make meaningful career shifts to transition from working for money to a career aligned with their astrological map.

This book brings together an encyclopaedic range of techniques focused on vocational astrology. It provides a systematic and easy to follow guide to building a complete astrological vocational profile which will illuminate and clarify the path to career and financial success.

[1. Astrology, Vocational. 2. Mind, Body, & Spirit. 3. Self-Help.]

Viktor Simon

Viktor Simon is an inspiring astrologer, with a rapidly growing international reputation. He blends modern, traditional and ancient methods in a unique way, achieving powerfully accurate results. Viktor is recognised as a gifted teacher. He has an enthusiastic and devoted community of students worldwide which includes both aspiring astrologers and experienced professionals.

In this book he brings together an encyclopaedic range of techniques focused on vocational astrology. It provides a systematic and easy to follow guide to building a complete astrological vocational profile which will illuminate and clarify the path to career success.

Visit astroviktor.com for more information on his services, his courses, and community membership options. Also explore the rich resource that is the Astro Viktor YouTube channel.

Foreword

The first time I met Victor in 2019 I asked him what his goal was. He looked me straight in the eyes and said: "To become the best Astrologer in the world."

I laughed and was startled by his boldness and confidence then, but he was dead serious. Just three years later, his mission statement is truly turning into a reality.

Victor is proving to be one of the best astrology teachers, mentors and practitioners.

I have watched his perfection driven work and progress with amazement. Never have I seen an astrologer create such a loyal student and client following in such a short time.

He works ceaselessly, juggling hundreds of students, webinars, readings, and constant research, while creating websites and video content! And now Victor's wisdom is coming in a written book! I could not be more excited to have some of his most pioneering research and knowledge in a book!

What I love the most about Victor, is his innovative approach to astrology! Combining ancient and new knowledge, a lot of which is his own findings too, through the thousand of charts he reads yearly. Like a visionary Sagittarius-Aquarius, he is seeing patterns and creating a truly unique system out of these!

There is no one more progressive, prolific and insightful on the astrology horizon now than Victor, he must be one of the ancient astrology sages reborn...that is the only way I can rationally explain to myself his unique talent in astrology and the secrets of the soul!

—Astrolada

Introduction

Vocational astrology is really important. People consult astrologers more often about careers than any other subject, even more than relationships. There is a good reason: we spend 40% of our lives at work and so making sure we are working in the optimal environment is crucial to our overall happiness in life.

These ideas were first brought together just after the Saturn-Jupiter conjunction at the end of 2020. The Great Conjunction which happens every 20 years is always connected to development in your career life. However, it also marks a transition to Jupiter-Saturn conjunctions in air signs, which hasn't happened since mediaeval times. Now, we will all be re-envisioning how we work in a radical way.

The astrological birth chart is a blueprint of potentials for this lifetime. It reflects karmic commitments we made before we were born. It reflects the challenges and opportunities we can engage in as our soul evolves through this incarnation experience. In this book we extract the salient career information, allowing you to write your own 'Mission Statement', much in the way a company creates a mission statement that commits to certain values, priorities, and objectives. Such clarity is invaluable as we navigate our working lives and allows us to most fully and rewardingly share our unique gifts with the world.

In this book we build up a detailed analysis of the Midheaven, and crucially, examine how that resonates with the Ascendant and Rising Sign. The 38 possible Midheaven and Rising sign combinations are explored in detail. We also examine the definitive influence of the Sun and Moon positions, as these 'guiding lights' influence every aspect of life. We look at the relationship between Saturn and Jupiter in the chart, then add in a number of other important factors to give a fully rounded, nuanced portrait of your optimal career choices: what you need to keep in mind to succeed. We identify the key players; the planets that are the drivers of your career success. Most importantly, we also explore the potential blocks and barriers to overcome and consider how that might be achieved.

This book outlines a blending of modern, traditional and ancient techniques. In the 'Whole Sign' house system, most of these techniques work for any house system you choose. Using the Whole Sign house system, however, gives the added information, because it shows the Midheaven (and Ascendant, IC and Descendant) as 'floating points' not tied to a house cusp. Everything is explained so it can be applied by the beginning astrology student but there is much here to interest the intermediate or advanced student too. We are mindful to revisit the basics here: angles, quadrants, the elements and modes of angles and planetary placements are all highly significant.

Every chart feature contributes to your particular 'temperament' as described by the 17th century English astrologer William Lilly. We include his method for calculating this characterisation of your personality and approach so you have another valuable tool for making the most positive life choices. In understanding a planetary placement, we go beyond signs and houses, by identifying decans and duads to give the fullest possible understanding. Then we add factors such as the Zenith, the possible influence of planetary declinations and the true effects of birth chart aspects. These are just some of the astrological tools we will lay out and clearly explain to empower you to create the ultimate astrological vocational profile.

Table of Contents

Understanding the Angles

The astrological birth chart has a basic structure: Two axes and four 'Compass Points'. These four points are the anchor points of the chart and are very important. These are the pillars which define the fundamental architecture of your chart, the 'energetic skeleton'. The Midheaven is one of the angles.

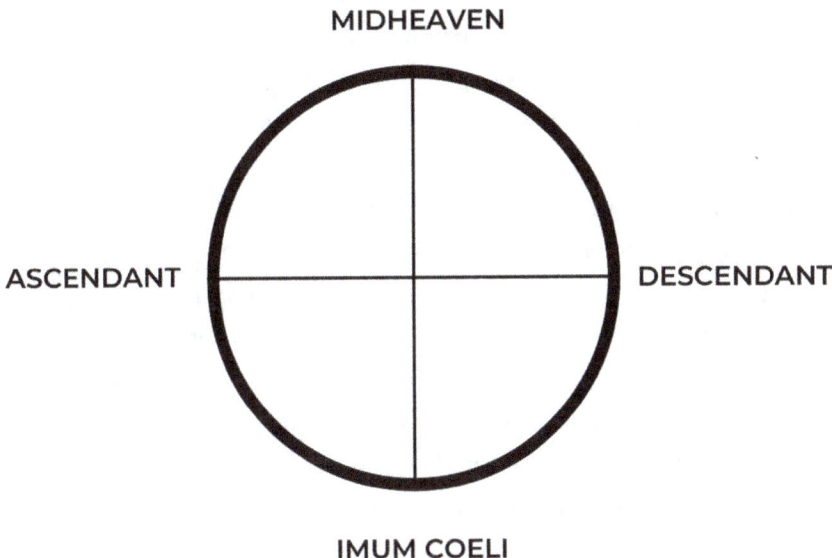

MIDHEAVEN

ASCENDANT

DESCENDANT

IMUM COELI

To the east (the left of your chart: east and west are different on celestial and terrestrial maps) is the Ascendant or Rising Sign (AC). This describes your personality, attitudes and approach to life. It can also indicate things about your physical appearance. Planets that closely aspect the AC also define your personality, adding nuance to the Rising Sign. The Rising Sign describes character traits. However, the Ascendant is not exactly 'who we are'. It is like a mask or persona we adopt rather than who we truly are. It is heavily influenced by parental expectations, teachers and others who told us who we *should* be: Ascendant to a large degree is conditioned or taught. Consider a Cancerian being told to stop crying, an Aries not to fight or a Taurean to hurry up: all very jarring to the spirit. You can think of the AC as your 'coping mechanism' for dealing with life. It is how we *appear* in the world.

The AC relates to free will.

The Midheaven (MC, Medium Coeli or 'Middle of the Sky') at the top of the chart is the point which indicates where you should be aiming for in life.

Like a 'CV' it describes the best version of yourself. Of course, most people are not operating at this level of perfection all the time. It is the 'reputation' point; describing where you need to be recognised and respected publicly. It is a descriptor for the life path.

The MC is 'who we are when we know people are watching'.

We need to find a way for the Ascendant *and* the Midheaven to be expressed in our work life. These can be harmonious or contradictory and so more problematic. Suppose, for example, a person has a Leo Midheaven and needs a stage, a place to shine and be admired; suppose however they also have a Scorpio rising sign, which has a more private, secretive and 'behind the scenes' energy. It will be more challenging for them to fully express the Leo Midheaven potential.

The IC (Imum Coeli-Bottom of the Sky) is the point opposite to the MC. It talks about your roots and origins, where you came from and how you were raised. It describes family patterns that influence you.

The IC can give insights into the things which might hold you back from achieving the promise and ambition of the MC; the fears, insecurities and deficiencies to be overcome. The IC is often overlooked, but I say, ignore the IC at your peril, it is the foundation of your chart. It is one of the places to explore to understand the blocks you encounter in career development.

The IC says something about our core self, our hidden motivations and who we secretly aspire to be. It also speaks to our heritage and who we were taught to be. It describes the emotional baggage we carry. It is who you are when you are alone; or you as a child.

The MC and IC axis is a definitive key to your work life: family life will inevitably affect your work life and vice versa. The Ascendant-Descendant axis will also exert a powerful influence. Astrology is always informed by polarities.

Finally, the Descendant or DC is the point directly opposite the Ascendant. The Descendant is well known for describing our relationship patterns and partners, but it is valuable also in pointing out the qualities that we don't acknowledge or recognise in ourselves. After all, relationships hold up a mirror to us, indicating things about us that we might not want to acknowledge; unintegrated aspects of the self. If we identify and own our Descendant traits this will prevent them undermining our success.

These angles are the basic parameters, the 'backbone' of your horoscope and, as such, are very strong and functional points in the chart. For this reason, we acknowledge a wide sphere of influence to them. We use an 'orb' of 5-8 degrees for aspects to the angles. For a conjunction, an orb of up to 10 degrees will show effects. Of course, the tighter the aspect, the more powerful the effect.

Quadrants

The first quadrant or first three houses of the chart, introduced by the Ascendant, describes us setting out on our 'hero's journey' of development and expression in life.

The second quadrant, covering houses four to six, is where we gain our security. It is introduced by the IC which describes our roots, origins, family and ancestral background. It reflects 'what we know', our 'comfort zone'.

The Descendant, leading the third quadrant is often identified with significant others. However, in terms of career it can also be seen as describing unintegrated aspects of our own psyche, personal characteristics we display but do not recognise and tend to project onto others, so it could be an insight into the blocks to our career progression.

For example, I was surprised when a friend pointed out that I could be judgemental and critical to others. I had always identified strongly with my kind, compassionate Pisces Ascendant, but when I asked, other friends agreed that I showed my Virgoan 'nit-picking' Descendant qualities on occasion also. I hadn't wanted to see that side of myself. So, we can look at this third quadrant, introduced by the Descendant as describing our dark or villainous energies, things we tend not to accept about ourselves. Fixing or accommodating, certainly recognising our Descendant optimises our approach (the Ascendant opposite) and thus contributes to career success.

The MC leads to our fourth and final quadrant, that of the 'guides' or more spiritual and transpersonal aspects of self. The MC is the key career indicator. We will delineate how to do a detailed MC breakdown in this book.

We need to examine the balance of planets in each quadrant. Which is the most 'tenanted' quadrant? This will be another career indicator.

The angles also have a planetary quality:
- The Ascendant has a Mars quality, regardless of the sign.
- The IC has the quality of the Moon.
- The Midheaven is solar, having the qualities of the Sun.
- The Descendant will have Venusian qualities.

The MC-IC Polarity

Consider the IC the roots of the tree and the MC as the branches, the flourishing point.

The MC calls us to leave our roots and family. The IC describes the soil around the tree that has nurtured our growth (or not). IC is where we come from and the MC is where we blossom in society. The quality of the soil determines the quality of the flourishing. You must understand, respect and 'feed' your IC appropriately to succeed in your career.

Remember the IC has that Lunar/Moon quality: it describes our habits developed in childhood, our deep primary needs and what we need to feel secure.

Career success depends on striking a balance between leaving the past behind to strike out on one's own and make one's own success without forgetting where we came from. Cutting ourselves off from the roots completely is disastrous to the tree.

The MC(Midheaven) point is the first line of our Career Mission Statement. It defines our vision of success and begins the story of how we have chosen to make the evolutionary journey of expressing our Sun (our true spiritual self) while honouring our roots (IC).

As well as its Solar flavour, the MC also has a Saturnian quality. It takes time to carefully formulate, develop, build and finally express the 'best version of ourselves' to share with the world.

The MC and IC are also, of course, the parental axis of the chart and understanding those familial influences will be very important. We work with the IC by understanding how to 'leave the nest' and take necessary risks, negotiating with our desire for the safety of 'what we know'. When we work with our MC, we become clear and explicit about what we want for ourselves, independent but cognisant of family expectations.

The IC is 'our womb and our tomb', and can indicate subconscious motivations and the roots of some of our ambitions and desires.

In every case it is vital to factor in all the angular influences. It is a common mistake to focus too much on one angle and then overlook the other energies influencing progress and achievement.

A clear view of the angular outlooks, blended with the influence of the Sun and the Moon, adding the Nodes of the Moon gives us a good basis for building a Vocational Profile.

Character of the Angles

Planets that are close to these compass points are termed 'Functional Planets'. It means their influence is magnified: they are typically 20% more powerful than they would be elsewhere in the chart. The angles are points of power.

By close to the angles, we mean within 10 degrees, that is we are using a 10 degree 'orb' or area of influence; the closer the placement, the stronger the planet's power. This 10-degree orb is not arbitrary. It was demonstrated by a French statistician and psychologist, called Michel Gauquelin who conducted extensive research into astrological factors in the 1920s. He was expecting to disprove astrological methods, but in fact found a 'Mars Effect' with that planet, when in proximity to the angles within 10 degrees correlated with particular strengths and capabilities in his subjects.

The planets which are placed near the angles of our chart are empowered to play a strong role in determining our 'life mission' (should we choose to accept it!).

In my chart, Uranus is conjunct my MC. This indicates that my career would ideally have a Uranian quality. In modern astrological rulership, Uranus is the ruler of astrology and that is my chosen profession. Equally, someone with Uranus on the MC might decide to be an electrician, electricity being another Uranian commodity.

The Angles and the Elements
The Ascendant: The Fire Angle

The ascendant is a Fire angle. The 'Natural Zodiac' places Aries, a fire sign, at the cusp of the first house: Aries is the 'natural' ruler of the first house, although of course a natal chart can have any of the twelve actual rising signs.

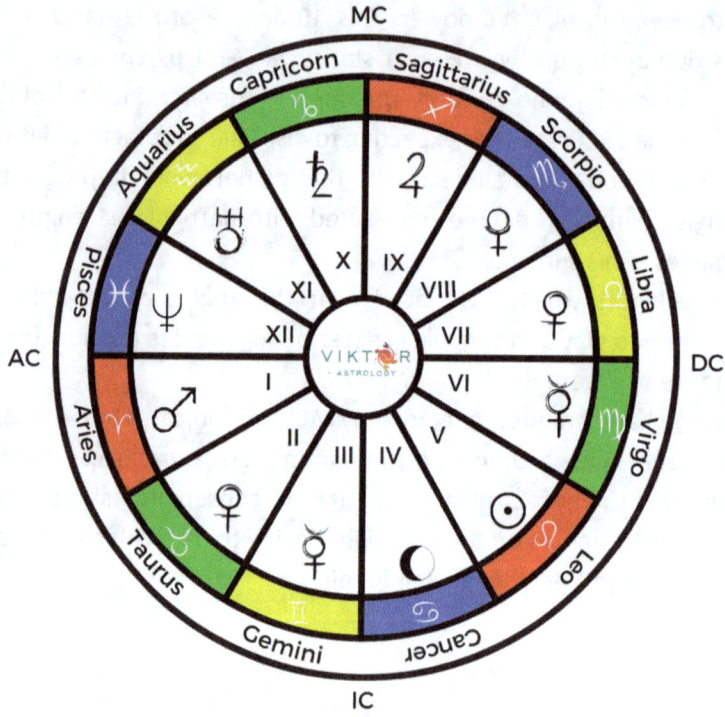

The Rising Sign is hugely important, because it shows where free will operates in your chart. It is the point on the Eastern horizon on the left-hand side of the chart. The Ascendant describes what you like and don't like. The Midheaven might indicate an optimal life direction, but this may not correspond to what the Ascendant shows you want to do. The Midheaven might be termed 'what the Gods plan for you' and then the Ascendant is what you decide. The Ascendant shows your human free will in action. Ancient astrologers equated the MC with 'God's Plan' for us; the AC is our (free will) plan. We make plans and the Gods laugh!

The MC (and IC) points on a chart also correlate to parental influences. So sometimes it happens that the MC describes what a parent thinks you ought to do, believing it to be for your best interests, but you might have other ideas. Parental expectations frequently have a huge influence on career choices. They might want you to be an accountant, but you want to be a dancer and there is conflict if parents cannot accept and respect dance as a career choice. It is vital to understand the influence of family. They give you your first ideas of success. Also, if the family is hindered by failing behaviours or unable to embrace change, that is inevitably part of your make-up too. It must be understood consciously, so it does not undermine you subconsciously. Consider how you can realistically make different choices and break barriers to success. It is not about rejecting your family or heritage, it is about taking a karmic point of view and deliberately activating success by bringing the MC and IC into balance. The ideal is to find a path that satisfies both the Ascendant and Midheaven objectives.

The Ascendant shows how the native makes decisions. For instance, I have a Pisces Rising Sign. Pisces is not a very decisive sign, but the decisions I do make tend to be based on emotional factors, because that is the nature of Pisces. Pisces considers feelings and impacts on others.

The Ascendant is your characteristic approach, your likes and dislikes and the persona you exhibit when you are out and about in the world. Remember, the Ascendant or Rising sign describes your personality and approach to life.

The IC: The Water Angle

The IC, your root, is what you have inherited, is your foundation in life. It will also describe you when you are alone and at home, as opposed to the Ascendant which describes you out and about in the world. The IC is the cusp of the fourth house of your chart ('naturally' ruled by Cancer and therefore a water house). It reveals your hidden motivations for what you hope to achieve in life. Many astrologers overlook the IC in regard to career issues, but it is really very important. To reiterate: Ignore the IC at your peril as it is showing what you secretly (really, really) want.

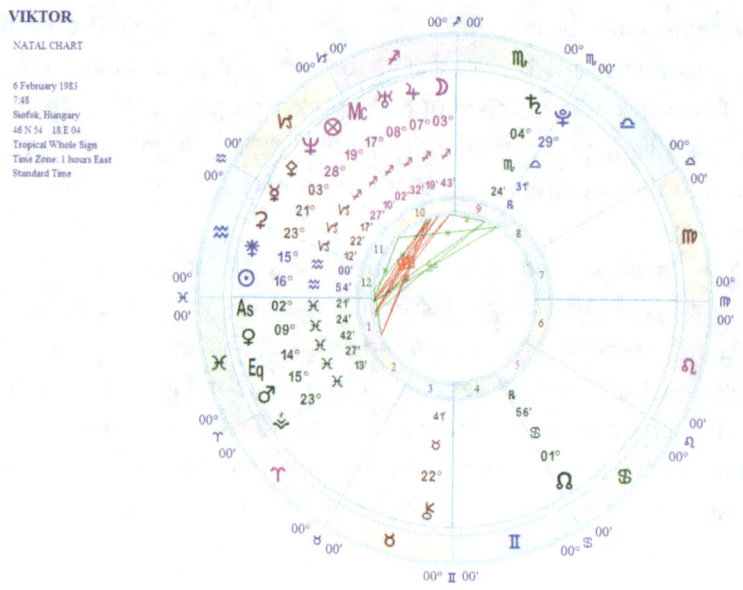

My chart has Gemini on the IC. I like to chat and communicate when I am alone—talking to myself or to my friends on the phone (Gemini rules technology too). The ruler of a Gemini IC is Mercury, which in my case is in Capricorn in the 11th house. This shows that I have a hidden motivation to achieve popularity (11th house) by teaching, perhaps (Mercury) and acquire social status (Capricorn), doing this in structured ways (Capricorn). Fourth house motivations are not those we freely share; we may be shy about them, fearing they will be misinterpreted or judged.

Once again, the secret desires of the IC are pitted against the free will decisions of the Rising Sign. In my case the Pisces Rising Sign ruler is Jupiter (by traditional rulership) and is in Sagittarius in the 10th house. The 10th house is about status and hierarchies and Sagittarius is also about teaching. So, in my case, the IC and Ascendant can be in agreement about the career direction.

Suppose, for example, in a chart the Rising Sign is Scorpio, ruled by Mars in the sixth house. Scorpio is an energy that is penetrating and seeks to understand deeply; it is forensic in approach. Mars in the sixth house wants to go into action in support of a cause. A sixth house placement indicates someone who wishes to render a service to others. A possible expression of this would be becoming a life coach (Scorpio insight, transformation) with a health focus (sixth house). A possible expression is being a personal trainer: Providing a service (6th house), with an active element (Mars / Aries) that is transformational (Scorpio). The personal approach would be very direct, outspoken, even con-frontational and challenging (Mars /Aries). Suppose also the IC hidden motivation is described in this case by Aquarius, with the ruler Saturn in the second house. This suggests that making serious (Saturn) money (2nd house) is a key motivation. The second house in this case is Sagittarius, so the objective is achieved in a Sagittarian way, perhaps by teaching, educating, traveling or communicating about spiritual values. There is an emotional need to satisfy the IC needs.

The Descendant: The Air Angle

The Descendant, of course, speaks of relationships. It also in a way speaks about the Law of Attraction: How, with the right attitude of positivity, you magnetically attract what and who you need to help you achieve in life.

In this chart example the ruler of the Descendant / and 7th house is Venus which is in the 7th in Taurus. This is what you are hoping to attract in this life. The seventh house position of the Descendant ruler emphasises the key importance of relationship to the native. Taurus indicates a desire for money, security and the earthy pleasures of sex, food and physical comfort.

In my chart the Descendant is Virgo, ruled by Mercury. Mercury is situated in the 11th house in Capricorn. Once again, the ruler of the 7th Descendant, showing what I need to attract, seems in accord with the Midheaven, Ascendant and IC aspirations. It is seeking popularity or fame (11th house) recognition and respect (Capricorn) via structured activity (Mercury in Capricorn) which could describe teaching.

The Midheaven: The Earth Angle

The MC speaks of achievement and reputation. It describes your goals and aims and what your success looks like. It talks about your highest potential. It also indicates how strongly you want to achieve success and provides clues as to how you might do it.

Ancient astrologers very strongly emphasised the Midheaven in a chart. Being strongly theistic, they believed that it showed 'the Will of God', and as such, not following the dictates of the Midheaven could bring retribution.

Consider Sagittarius on the 10th house cusp: Sagittarian energy is an energy of kingship, exaggeration and expansion. It wants to be the best, the most 'est' of everything. Certainly, it would suggest a desire for success and a big reputation. If instead, the MC had fallen in the adjacent Scorpio house, that would be very different. Scorpio is a hidden and secretive energy. It does not mean it does not seek success or leadership and achievement, but it is important to preserve a private life too. Scorpio doesn't need fanfare and red carpets in the same way.

The MC also points to how you achieve success and recognition. It is about how you reach your highest personal development. Astrologer Frank Clifford believes the MC will reflect your childhood aspirations. Even if these dreams were unrealistic, some vestiges will remain. For example, someone who wanted to be an astronaut might end up working in aviation or some other travel or air-element related career. Steven Forrest said the MC is what you want on your tombstone—as a defining aspect of your personal 'mission statement'.

The Midheaven most accurately describes you when you reach a midlife point of review, perhaps in the period aged 33 to 48. This is the point when we are typically looking back to see how far we have come and checking that we are developing in line with the goals and ambitions we have set for ourselves.

The first house describes the first 7 years of life and early development. After that, each house shows about 3.5 years. Thus, the 10th house is reflecting the life development at approximately 33-48. More advanced students will recognise this coincides quite closely with major astrological milestones like the Saturn Return and the Lunar Nodal Return.

Another analogy for understanding the four angles is to relate them to the times of day they represent. The Ascendant / Eastern Horizon is the Sunrise part of the chart. It reflects the self. The IC represents Midnight, it is secret, dark and hidden; it represents the inner, private, emotional self. It is the mysterious place where one day ends and another begins. The Descendant is Sunset; it is a point of relaxation, lowering energy and rest. The Midheaven is the midday point, the Sun is highest in the sky and this is your public most visible self.

Astrologers often like to play a game when they meet someone for the first time, trying to guess their Rising Sign. However, what is frequently most immediately obvious is in fact the Midheaven Sign. Imagine you are introduced to someone who appears with a perfect impressive hairstyle, adorned with stylish bling. This could very likely be a Leo Midheaven. As an astrologer you know there are only a few possible associated Rising Signs. The most likely one is the corresponding fixed sign of Scorpio. Closer examination might clue you into whether this is the case. The public image presents confidence and strutting self-expression (Leo), but the reality is hidden and darker and more intense (Scorpio). There is a proverb: 'The barking dog never bites': What you see is not what you get.

In my case I have a Pisces Rising Sign. My tenth house 'work self' is quite unlike the 'personal expression'. I have a stellium of five planets in my Sagittarian 10th house. A stellium indicates a strong concentration of energy in the career house, which will show a very serious focus on work and career. My Pisces Rising Sign likes to be a party animal, sing karaoke and let his hair down, my work colleagues would be surprised to see me when I am playing and 'being myself' as they usually see me in my MC career mode.

Planets on the Angles

Planets near the IC

Planets around the IC have a 'New Moon' energy. That means an energy of 'planting seeds' and nurturing them: coming up with a new idea and nurturing it through the first planning stages. People with a lot of planets around the IC are people who live in the moment. Thinking ahead and thinking things through is not their strength. Considering that a New Moon has no light at all: people operating from the planets here have to rely entirely on their instincts. A lot of planets on the IC can indicate quite a spiritual sort of person. They are very spontaneous and life for them is a big adventure. Adventures involve risk, so life could be quite a rocky path for these folks. Bear in mind that the seeds planted at the New Moon come to fruition at the Full Moon. What you are bringing from family influence (or even past lives -4th house) will be the basis of your success (10th). If the planets at the IC are challenging ones, this is not necessarily a negative; it indicates the need to 'make friends' with these presenting energies, because this will serve you well. Natives with challenging IC influences can be quite self-absorbed and focused on their own journey. Having lots of planets on the IC can also indicate the family or family issues hindering your progress.

Planets near the Ascendant

Planets at the Ascendant take on the character of the First Quarter Square Moon. People with planets on the Ascendant get tested in life. It is the energy of a square aspect: the person will have to act, and act quickly, in response to life tests. They are good at split second decision-making. To follow the seed analogy: at the Ascendant, the seeds planted at the IC are menaced by an approaching storm and the native will have to decide how to respond and protect them. It also speaks of shedding old patterns and creating new ones. Planets on the Ascendant people are pioneers and often the heroes and heroines in life.

Planets near the Midheaven

Planets near the Midheaven have the character of a Full Moon. They speak of maturity and success. These planets represent the pinnacle of what you can achieve in life. People with planets on the Midheaven are typically idealists, about all aspects of life. They search for a belief system they can adopt. They are people who make a 'splash' in some way. We will consider individual planets on the Midheaven in greater depth later in the book.

Planets near the Descendant

This is a Last Quarter Square Moon energy.

Planets on the Descendant ask the native to readjust. Being associated with the Descendant, it reflects how, in relationships, we are required to accommodate the needs of others. With planets on the Descendant, the native will be tested in the area of relationships. Without evolution, they will experience difficulties in this department. There is a sense here of leaving things behind and thinking of new beginnings. These natives need time and space to figure these things out and can seem to struggle with relating to the here and now: they are often pondering the past and possible future. Think of it as analogous to the stage where the caterpillar goes into the cocoon, in order to eventually become a butterfly.

The House and Sign of the Midheaven and Aspects to the Midheaven

The sign of the Midheaven and aspects to the Midheaven are going to indicate what will bring you success in life and personal fulfilment. Of course, what constitutes success is different for everyone. Success could be fortune, having a happy family, fame, or achieving something that you are remembered for; having a legacy of some kind. Every Midheaven sign describes a different motivation. We will analyse this motivation by considering the element and modality concerned.

House Placement
of the Midheaven

I use the Whole Sign house system. It works brilliantly for me, but I am not evangelical about it. You can apply almost every technique in this book using any house system.

One benefit of the Whole Sign house system here is that it generates a 'floating' Midheaven: the MC might be placed in 8th 9th 10th 11th or (very rarely) in the 12th house. In contrast other systems, such as Placidus or Porphyry, make the Midheaven always the cusp of the tenth house.

The Midheaven (MC) house position by itself gives an indication of possible professions, so if you use a whole sign system you will have this additional piece of information.

8th House MC

The 8th house MC could suggest a job working with other people, as long as the sign placement also supports this. It might be connected to an eighth house area such as the occult, investments, psychology or sexuality, or involve providing consultations. The eighth house is a money house and suggests providing a service in exchange for a fee. The work may involve money, either in terms of actually making money—being paid by others—or merely handling other people's money in some way in the course of one's work. Another eighth house resonance is for the work to be somehow transformational.

9th House MC

For a 9th house MC, the work would likely be to do with travel or teaching, the sharing of belief systems and in some way connecting to 'the gods within'. The 9th house is to do with The Divine, it is to do with an 'Olympian' outlook. In some way the 9th house MC expression is connected to significant teachings and sharing knowledge. The career path must have true meaning for the individual.

10th House MC

With a 10th house MC, the work is about gaining recognition, achieving something of significance and leaving a legacy behind you. It gives a very visible Success with a capital 'S'. 10th house MC people work hard and climb ladders and hierarchies.

11th House MC

For the 11th house MC, it is significant to build a community of some sort. In the modern world the 11th house represents the internet and social media. Previously, the 11th house has been considered the house of friends, but true friends are better represented by the 3rd house, in our everyday close environment. Eleventh house 'friends' are more like Facebook friends. Eleventh house MC people have to build a strong social network, and in our times, it can indicate that they should work on the internet. They work well in teams, potentially in an advisory capacity.

12th House MC

The 12th house is about service; not as in providing a service for profit (which is more typical of the 8th house) but in providing a service such as medicine, personal support or a charitable service. The 12th speaks of the underprivileged and the needy or weak and with an MC here, the native may be drawn to work with such people. The 12th house person of course should be paid, but not directly by the recipients of the service. 12th house MC people are motivated by a need to 'give back to the universe'.

Thus, the house positions of the MC give us one of the first clues as to what the best work for us will be.

Masculine and Feminine Planetary Energies and Correspondences

Aries	Masculine	Fire	1st house
Taurus	Feminine	Earth	2nd house
Gemini	Masculine	Air	3rd house
Cancer	Feminine	Water	4th house
Leo	Masculine	Fire	5th house
Virgo	Feminine	Earth	6th house
Libra	Masculine	Air	7th house
Scorpio	Feminine	Water	8th house
Sagittarius	Masculine	Fire	9th house
Capricorn	Feminine	Earth	10th house
Aquarius	Masculine	Air	11th house
Pisces	Feminine	Water	12th house

Notice all the Fire and Air signs are masculine and all the Earth and Water signs are feminine.

Consider whether there is a majority of masculine or feminine energy planets by noting their sign placement. This gives a further general clue about a suitable occupation.

A man with many feminine planets will not be able to 'recharge' easily. They will require more rest time and more alone time. They are not likely to choose a highly active typically masculine job e.g., being a racing car driver, they do not have the right sort of energy for it.

Conversely, a woman with a high level of masculine planetary energy will not be happy, sitting in a beauty salon or doing embroidery. They will need to find a more active career.

The masculine or feminine energy of the house placement of a planet can also influence this.

Midheaven Indications

Midheaven Indications-
A Summary:
What you stand for
What gives us a sense of success
Whether you want to be successful
Public perception of our lifestyle
Life direction
Parental themes:
  MC- Mother's influence;
  IC- Father's influence Inheritance
Our definition of success
Recognition
Early aspirations
Mission
Public Image
Relationship to authority
'What goes on our tombstone'

Note that on the 'parental axis' and the MC/IC designations, the Father is the 'foundation of the family' and traditionally the financial provider, so is assigned to the IC. We usually inherit the Father's name, so that belongs to the IC. The Christian name, therefore, is assigned to the Midheaven.

Signs and aspects to the Midheaven are going to more clearly describe the energies that bring success and we are coming to that.

Of course, success means different things to different people. It might be financial success or fame or respect or creating a legacy; a name that will live on.

Everyone has unique talents and potentials. Success is ultimately is a simple formula:

Determination + Courage + Hard Work = Success.

Astrology is brilliant at pointing out the combined energies to emphasise to achieve success.

The Midheaven is outlining the image we have to project in the world to meet our goals.

Compare this with the Moon sign, our innermost, private, emotional needs and see how much this is in alignment. If they are very contrary, that is a challenge we need to overcome.

The IC can also give us clues about what might hold us back from our MC image of success.

Elements on the Midheaven
Fire on Midheaven

With a Fire sign on the Midheaven you need competition and challenge and to be strongly motivated in your career. They are all about action, enthusiasm, drive and inspiration.

These people are feisty and need to be very active. They are instinctively self-promoting and highly proactive in seeking the right work for themselves. They have the character of the Choleric temperament.

Temperament refers to the 17th century concept of health and personality type relating to the relative balance of various bodily fluids or 'humours' within the body. Imbalances of the humours, namely blood, phlegm, yellow bile and black bile, were the root of illnesses. Those with a constitutional preponderance of blood were 'sanguine'; of yellow bile 'choleric', of black bile 'melancholic' and of phlegm 'phlegmatic'. These adjectives persist in English, describing various 'temperament' although the arcane medical philosophy is now disregarded.

Thus Fire MC people are 'choleric'. They need to win at all costs and feed their egos through their work activity. They require recognition and the opportunity to rise higher and higher.

These people also have the capacity to inspire and motivate others. They have 'fire in the belly' and are natural leaders. In doing this they are actually creating the challengers they personally need around them.

The sign of the ruler it is in can mitigate this attitude somewhat, e.g. If the ruler of the Fire Midheaven is placed in a Water sign, it will nuance the approach. Also, is this fiery MC in keeping with the overall elemental balance of the chart?

Fire MC people can benefit from the influence of all other elemental energies in restraining exaggerated risk taking. As they can easily get bored, a little Earth energy would help them with perseverance and follow through.

Fire:

Challenge Competition Excitement Risk Speed Self Promotion
Glory Triumph Winning Recognition

Air on the Midheaven

Air on the Midheaven is all about connectivity and the world of ideas. The right career for them will involve coming up with theories and ideas and discussing, analysing and evaluating these ideas with others. Talking activities and perhaps academics suit them. They have an essentially humanitarian approach. Knowledge, new learning and variety in the work is very important. They deal with the gathering, sharing and analysis of data at all levels. They can benefit from fire energies—from their own chart or via partners to fully manifest their ideas. They should seek out variety and fast paced environments and 'Communicate, coordinate and collaborate'. This corresponds to a Sanguine temperament.

Air:

Knowledge Ideas Theory Humanity
Travel Interaction Variety Analysis

Earth on the Midheaven

With Earth on the Midheaven the motivation is one of money, financial security and stability. An Earth sign is not likely to change jobs unless another (better) one is lined up. They will not take risks of being without money or unable to meet their responsibilities. The focus will be on security and the 'bottom line'. They need solid, tangible results from their work activity that demonstrate their worth. They are happy in a work environment governed by routine and clear structures and hierarchies. It's natural for business; they come up with a limited number of ideas, but these will be good, solid and practical ones. It's a common sense MC. They should embrace routine, steady progress, maintenance and consistency.

Work involving the actual physicality of the body is suitable for Earth Midheaven People. They can benefit from Fire energy influences for inspiration, raised optimism and encouragement to take measured risks. This corresponds to a Melancholic temperament.

Earth:

Security Stability Money Self-Worth Tangible Results
Routine Steady Income Structure Building Things Body

Water on the Midheaven

Water on the Midheaven makes emotion and the world of feelings the central priority. They need to really enjoy their work or they will suffer. They need to make emotional connections and bonds with others through their job, whether with clients or colleagues or bosses. They are 'people-people'. Great areas for them are healing activities, being carers, advisors or therapists—or 'saving' people. They can greatly benefit from having a stable 'grounded' partner in their career. It is a personal humanitarian energy. Water on the MC relates to a Phlegmatic temperament.

Fire and Air energies are 'masculine' and outward-directed. They are 'hot' energies. People with these elements on the MC need to be more extroverted, upward directed and people-facing.

Earth and Water energies are 'feminine', introverted and downward-directed. People with these elements on the MC gravitate to support roles. If they find themselves in leadership positions, they do with a 'right hand man or woman'.

Water:

Emotions, Working with People, Making Emotional Bonds, Healing, Caring, Counselling

---

Elemental Imbalance
Across the Chart

An overall elemental imbalance across the chart can indicate problems too. For example, with a low Earth representation in the chart, the person might show a general failure to manifest their ideas and visions. They might be insufficiently attentive to money matters or overspend or be hoarders (attempting to 'ground themselves with stuff'). They need to systematically address these tendencies, for instance by learning good financial management and by saving and investing.

Modality on the Midheaven

Modality of the MC indicates the amount of change a person needs, desires or tolerates in their career.

For instance, a mutable MC will have at least two work profiles in life and these will often be quite unrelated roles. Fixed MC signs resist change and Cardinal MCs will want more variety, with change being motivated by frustration with slow progression in the first field.

Cardinal

Cardinal energy indicates leadership roles.

This is the energy of the signs Cancer, Libra, Capricorn and Aries, each showing a different type of leadership.

Aries wants to win, wants to 'wear the crown'.

Cancer wants to lead a 'family'; they will win hearts as well as minds. Libra is about leading in partnership with another or a group of others.

Capricorn is focused on achievement, doing a task and putting their stamp on it. They earn their leadership position by inspiring respect for their hard work and commitment.

All Cardinal signs want to be visible and recognised for something:

Cancer wants to be the Best Mum Ever; Libra the Best Partner Ever, etcetera.

All cardinal signs are 'go-getters' who thrive on challenge. They respond well to change, implementing whatever is required; they are great in emergencies and under pressure.

Fixed

Fixed energies are all about principles and rules. They are *very* strict about rules.

They want schedules and to know what happens when. Routine and 9-5 are great for them. Uncertainty unsettles them. They hold onto things in life and can be a tad stubborn. Their focus is power and principles.

Fixed signs include Taurus, Leo, Scorpio, and Aquarius.

Taurus, probably the most stubborn of all, holds onto money most especially.

Leo holds onto fame.

Scorpio holds onto power.

Aquarius holds onto principles.

Mutable

The Mutable Signs are Gemini, Sagittarius, and Pisces. They are concerned with gathering knowledge. A mutable sign on the Midheaven often indicates multiple paths. It is easy for them to change lifestyles and careers. They value knowledge and freedom. They need to *learn* at work. They look for ways to reinvent themselves.

I have a Sagittarius MC and sharing knowledge is my career. Freedom is very important to me. I can't be bored. I need to learn all the time.

Mutable-sign people make quick decisions and quick moves.

Imagine a chart with a Scorpio Midheaven (Fixed Water): Scorpio could be about finance perhaps. It is most surely about Power. Water is about making emotional bonds and connecting with others. It suits careers like therapy, counselling and caring for others: element and Modality alone are already suggesting directions.

This individual needs Power (Scorpio) and Emotion (Water). Perhaps they could work in a job where emotions are transformed (Scorpio). They could be an energy healer or a therapist.

Suppose the Rising Sign is Aquarius: Then we incorporate a need for principles.

Scorpio is about digging deep (e.g., finding out about a person's emotions). The Aquarian Ascendant holds on to (fixed energy), analyses (air) and applies the Scorpio knowledge in a humanitarian, principled (Aquarian) way.

The MC is ruled by Mars which is in the first house. The first house speaks of personal development.

Aquarius is humanitarian, Mars in Aquarius will stand up and fight for those weaker than himself.

One possibility would be to work with others, helping them to overcome emotional difficulties, perhaps situations of crisis (e.g., crisis intervention counselling) or doing energy healing on their bodies in order to give people a sense of freedom.

The idea here is not to be prescriptive, but to play with the possibility of the energies to find a range of career expressions that would fit, by analysing the energies which are interacting.

Using Decans and Duads

Every sign on the chart comprises 30 degrees. Decans divide the sign into three 10° segments. The decan where an angle or planet resides gives further nuance to the nature of the sign placement.

In the first decan, the characteristics of the sign are shown most purely: the first third of a house has the quality of the sign on the cusp doubly emphasised.

Being in the second decan adds the underlying quality of the *next sign in the same element* as the sign on the cusp.

The third decan shows the influence of the *subsequent sign in the same element*.

In this way, the first decan of a Cancer is 'purely Cancerian'; the second decan is Cancerian with the flavour of Scorpio (the next water sign) and the third decan Cancerian with the flavour of Pisces (the subsequent water sign).

Considering the sign and the decan of an angle or planet gives greater depth to our understanding.

Duads (also written dwads) add another layer of nuance. Duads are a degree-placement system used in Vedic astrology since the 15th or 16th century. A decan might be considered as having 4 segments of 2.5 degrees; the first 2.5 degrees have the quality of the decan and each subsequent 2.5 degrees the quality of the subsequent zodiacal sign:

e.g.: Decan is Aries

1st 2.5 degrees Aries (1st duad)

2nd 2.5 degrees Taurus (2nd duad)

3rd 2.5 degrees Gemini (3rd duad)

4th 2.5 degrees Cancer duad (4th duad)

This system is highly dependent on the accuracy of the chart, so if you are going to use duads, you *must* rectify the chart.

Rectification

Especially with a 29° rising sign, it is necessary to rectify. I use pictures to rectify—pictures of the person in every decade of life. William Lilly the 17th century astrological master similarly used appearances to rectify charts.

I consider that using the timing of relationships, also marriage or even babies as many doto rectify charts, are not accurate because these things are *processes*.

An accident, however, gives a precise date.

Signs on the MC and the 38 Midheaven and Rising Sign Combinations

In this section we examine the Midheaven signs and the 38 possible combinations of Midheaven and Rising Sign individually. This unique resource will give a strong basis to the delineation of the path of success.

Remember: the MC shows your tools for success. The IC, the polarity that we always need to consider, shows what you have been taught. Of this, use only what you really need and what genuinely serves you. The MC is not directing one to a specific job, it is describing the traits, energies and behaviours to embrace for optimal success.

If the analysis given here does not resonate here—especially if we are dealing with early or late degrees on the angles, the timing of the chart may be off and rectification would be a good idea. A few minutes difference can change the sign on the Ascendant or the MC.

Aries Midheaven

With an Aries MC, we are dealing with Cardinal Fire. Cardinal speaks of leadership and being in Charge. Fire speaks of Achieving. Mere challenging tasks are not enough for an Aries MC, they require competition. They love attention, must be recognised and be seen as 'Number One' at all costs.

They will sweep away anyone or anything in the path of their goals, so it's not a good thing to stand in their way. They are also good at urging on others; in doing this they are fostering the competition they crave. Doing things faster and better is part of this competitive attitude. Aries MC sets the pace. They are pioneers, where they are the first to dare, others follow: they break new ground. It's great for entrepreneurs. They need to be forthright; to declare their intentions. They are born warriors and it is their birthright is to fight—and win! Short-term challenge is their ideal environment. Looking at the sign and house placement of the MC ruler is going to indicate the particular sphere of activity.

Aries MC secretly fears not being liked and being lonely. Consider that the IC opposite is in Libra, which is all about connecting with others. The IC that opposes the MC will always highlight where you might fail. Aries MC feels they have failed if they are indecisive or if they rely too much on partners or others (these are Libra's negative traits). Libran imperatives to collaborate and share equally are somehow taught to the native in their formative environment, but they won't be happy or fulfilled in that sort of scenario. They need to strike out and act on their own desires, but be mindful not to express negative Arian traits (e.g. by following the rules / the law and not being overly aggressive in interactions).

Arian energy is active and masculine. Being physically active and literally using the muscles can be a great expression, for example as a sportsperson.

To succeed they would benefit from being pushing and developing, to some extent, egoistic characteristics—unapologetically. It's who they are.

Aries MC Traits

Interests: sports, competition, sexuality, adventure, beginnings, conquering

Roles: leadership, army, warrior, advocate, pioneering, motivation, bully, athlete, initiator, competitor

Positive traits: brave, courageous, pioneering, daring, motivational, energetic, enthusiastic, dynamic, determined, adventurous, extroverted, bold, heroic, self-starting, driven

Negative traits: aggressive, quick-tempered, pushy, rash, impatient, domineering, inconsiderate, arrogant, impulsive

Aries MC and Cancer Rising

Bear in mind, our objective is always to find a 'solution' or path or job that satisfies both the MC and the Rising Sign. Here the MC qualities conflict with the Cancerian nature of shyness and emotional sensitivity.

Aries is about competition. Cancer is all about protection. So, you might take the lead in doing something that protects others, for example, coming to the aid of others. Actually, with two Cardinal energies, there is a very strong emphasis on being in charge. Cancer is instinctive and focused on what they *feel* is right or wrong. Cancer might typically take the lead in working with children; Aries leads in sport; so, one possibility is being a great sports teacher. Aries is about fighting for others. Cancer, ruled by the Moon, needs to connect emotionally with people. Aries would be great fighting for peoples' rights. Cancer focuses on protecting the vulnerable. Cancer rules children and families. So, a role protecting the rights of children or families would be an ideal expression.

Other possible career options are being a family counsellor or working in social services or child protection; advocacy roles are ideal. Perhaps being a firefighter (Aries: fire and valour; Cancer: saving others. Working in the police or in rescue services would be fulfilling. Animal rescue would work here too. Cancer is associated with property, so hospitality careers like being a chef or hotelier satisfy. Entertainment roles such as acting, dancing and being a performer, or a talent promoter would work.

To get a more nuanced description, we need to examine the MC ruler sign and position.

e.g., an Aries Midheaven ruler (Mars) situated in Gemini gives a very mentally curious sort of Mars and so modifies the profile.

Possibilities: Family Counsellor, Social Services, Firefighter, Chef, Hotelier, Surgeon, Hospitality Management, Actor, Entertainer, Dancer, Promoter.

Aries MC and Leo Rising

Here we have two fire elements, both very 'go-getter' energies. Leo Rising wants to be somehow on the stage and grabbing attention. Aries *fights* for this attention and conceptualises this as a competition. This is a combination very driven to succeed. Both are seeking to win and achieve victory and fame, so a public aspect to their job is key. An element of danger might be a bonus too. Leo is focused on creative self-expression and the Aries encourages this in the self and in others. Writing, painting or blogging are examples of expressive work. Diaries and autobiographies are good outlets for these energies, these people probably lead exciting lives with tales to tell! Aries brings in competition—they might compete, for instance, in a talent show. Being a racing driver works for this combo too because it is competitive and dangerous but also flashy with lots of glamourous focus on the daring driver. It is a good combination for an athlete: Aries gives speed and the taste for competition. Leo, as a fixed energy, gives strength and endurance.

Aries is pioneering; Leo has a flair for the dramatic. Aries is about the ego; Leo needs to express that ego in a creative way.

Possibilities: Actor, Racing Driver, Reality TV, TV Presenter, Talent Shows, Athlete.

Aries MC and Gemini Rising

Gemini's focus is on youth, communication and gathering information. It is highly versatile and adaptive and loves new things. Sharing information is brilliant for them. They love talking! Find these folks 'talking a blue streak".

Aries is very impatient and needs new experiences too or they get bored. Connecting with people out and about and being continually exposed to new things is great for them.

Possibilities: Teacher, Youth Worker, Investigative Journalism, Computer Programming, Engineer, Typist, Media Analyst, Brain Surgeon, Crime Reporter, Model, Catwalk Work.

Taurus Midheaven

Taurus Midheaven works with what is tangible. Money is important to them and they must have financial security or safety nets. It is vital for them to value what they do and they are keen to value what others do as well. They are an Earth energy and as such move and achieve slowly and steadily. Taurus loves food or anything to do with the senses: touch (e.g., massage); speaking or singing. Ruled by Venus, there is an artistic quality to Taurean energy. They like the good things in life. Art, beauty and anything relating to harmony belongs to Taurus.

They like to be comfortable and like to move steadily, appreciating clear plans and schedules. They shouldn't be rushed or intimidated by others. They will achieve, by being their natural selves and being patient. It is good for them to spend money on themselves, look good, eat well and show their achievements to others. This builds their self-worth.

They are good at 'taking care of the pennies so the pounds take care of themselves'. Another trait is being really good listeners. They support others, but are themselves very self-contained with their own value system.

Taurus MC has to enjoy their work. It is a Venusian sign, so it has artistic and creative qualities. They might express that in music, food, art, massage or gardening; and approach this in a way that is steady, fixed and reliable. For example, they might run a food business, but take care to invest in the very best equipment which pays for itself in time through efficiency and reliability.

The corresponding IC will be Scorpio; thus, they are scared of sudden change, crisis and situations without a sense of trust. Relying on others financially would really disturb them, they need to create their security for themselves. Their early environment typically taught them to be acutely focused on power: potentially they experienced a background of high intensity, power struggles and addictions, obsessions or control drama.

They walk on eggshells and build strong defences that actually do not serve them in later life. They need to examine the power issues of their family background and ask how this has influenced them. They may find that a tendency to control others and focus too much on societal status, or succumbing to unreasonable distrust and jealousy undermines their potential for personal success.

It helps if they surround themselves with people who build their self-esteem. They are very faithful, favouring long-term, committed relationships and serving long apprenticeships.

They succeed by staying close to nature. Gardens and the natural world are their proper arena. Succumbing to their tendency to laziness and over-indulgence will undermine their success so they need to be able to find motivation to persevere within themselves.

Taurus MC Traits

Interests: finance, making a living, security, sensual pleasures, earth things, conservation, holding onto things, principles, traditions
Roles: finance, money management, investment, gardening, food related, nature
Positive traits: practical, down to earth, sensible, value others, stable, endurance, easy going, patient, hard-working
Negative traits: stubborn, old-fashioned, closed to new ideas, self-indulgent, hoarding, lethargic, lazy, possessive, materialistic, predictable, unbending

---

Remember MC is what the world sees; the AC is what we want others to see.

Taurus MC and Leo Rising

These two energies are both very artistic. Leo loves the stage and Taurus loves singing, so being a singer would be a great expression of these energies.

Leo relates to hobbies, so Taurean hobbies, that is activities relating to art, beauty and the natural world might be transitioned into careers. Taurus MC with Leo rising needs to do work they deeply enjoy. Leo is about display and Taurus is about principles or values, so they need to do work that demonstrates their personal values. Donald Trump has this MC / AC combination. Whatever you feel about him politically, he is keen to be seen as loyal (Leo) to his country and as a person rigidly adhering to his principles. Both Leo and Taurus are fixed energies, not changing easily. In fact, they can be stubborn. The opposing fixed angle is Scorpio/Aquarius. They are focused on security and any sort of insecurity is going to destabilise them.

Possible careers are as artists and entertainers, dancers, fashion designer's stylists, hairdressers, make-up artists, film directors, brand image creatives or managers, perhaps working in a theatre. As Leo relates to children, running a children's drama group is a possibility. The creativity needs to come out with this combination.

Possibilities: Musician, Entertainer, Dancer, Artist, Fashion Designer, Brand Image Manager, Stylist, Hairstylist, Makeup Artist, Film Director, Garden Designer.

Taurus MC and Cancer Rising

Cancer is about protecting and caring for others, creating a safe environment for people. Taurus is also keen to create comfort and security around them. Taurus has a focus on self-worth. Cancer can relate to the body, as it is ruled by the Moon. Above all, Cancer wants to nurture others. Taurus is interested in food among other things. These folks need to find work where they become a pillar for others. They want to support others, whether by building their confidence or supporting others with food; giving people a security blanket in some way.

Taurus as a fixed energy, holds on to things; Cancer is about emotions; there can be difficulties letting go of people here.

Possibilities: Chef, Pâtissier, Cake Decorator, Baker, Environmental Protection, Gardener, Agriculture, Caretakers, Life Insurance, Nurse, Care- home Worker, Interior Designer, Security Industry, Property Management, Real Estate.

Taurus MC and Virgo Rising

Virgo has an association with craft. People with this combination need to identify a craft they are attracted to and work to become masters of that craft. Focus in this way avoids the scattering of energies (failing to see the wood for the trees) that can plague Virgo influence. Virgo and Taurus are both Earth energies. They need order, schedule and routine. They are both naturally reliable and hard-working. People can count on them. Neither of them seeks the spotlight as they are quite shy. They are probably happier working in the background. They can still be strong leaders, but will lead from the background. Virgo is interested in service to others and Taurus is about building things, so they need to build something that is of service to others, especially if there is an artistic quality to it (Taurus) and if there is the need to focus on details (Virgo). In fact, attention to detail is a key to career success here, especially in their own business.

Possibilities: Financial advisors, Financial Managers, Debt Management, Music Teachers, Composers, Typists, Data Entry Specialists, PAs, Nutritionists, Animal Welfare Workers, Veterinarians, Herbalists.

Gemini Midheaven

Here we are in the world of communications, social media and connecting to others. Gemini MC has *lots* of interests and multiple talents, so possible expressions are endless. Gemini is a mutable energy and Gemini MC can easily jump from one career to another. They need mental stimulation and cannot stand to be bored. They need a constant stream of new ideas and people around them they get along with. They need to express wit and humour and have a degree of mobility. They are the original social butterflies. Gemini does have a need for freedom and does not like to be restricted by schedules and such. They might even have a 'dual persona' or two names even (two 'handles', or nicknames). They might juggle two jobs or two businesses.

They are good at spotting patterns. They gather information, facts and data, and communicate what they learn. They are here to build bridges, act as agents and make short journeys (for instance, traveling from client to client). They will want to be continually learning and updating their information, as well as have the latest technology and communications systems and tools.

They are good at exploring different points of view and listening and understanding the needs of others. This helps them excel in business situations. They need to be creating relationships, using wit and humour and they won't be happy behind a desk. They are curious and their super-powers are adaptability and versatility.

The big fear for a Gemini MC (consider the opposing Sagittarian IC) is being judged, being considered out of touch, not up to date or not being needed or valuable to others. It suggests formative experiences underpinned by strong religious, philosophical or moral codes. The volume of information available and generated today, which they cannot resist, can be overwhelming for them. They might feel insecure around education and knowledge, feeling they never know enough, with the associated danger of becoming an 'eternal student' and never going on to teach which is the place they would excel. They could find themselves self-censoring communications, whether in speech or email.

It is possible parents expected them to live out their parents' own dreams, or pushed them to operate on a world stage when their true path was more local. It is typical for a Sagittarius IC to leave home very early, possibly escaping to a marriage they regret, returning to the parental home and getting stuck there.

They succeed when they ensure they are continuously developing themselves and their ideas. Gemini is happy if they are learning. They need to prioritise the practical over the philosophical and avoid being hemmed in by a particular belief system. It's helpful for them to continually 'interview' others to renew their knowledge and ideas. They fail if they worry too much about 'losing their freedom' or if they insist on being right. Repetitive tasks and activities are fatal to them.

On the plus side they are naturally positive and optimistic.

Gemini MC Traits

Interests: fideas, learning, courses, reading, writing, talking, handcraft

Roles: agent, communicator, messenger, bridge builder, information, data, speaker, writer, presenter, jack-of-all-trades

Positive traits: communicative, persuasive, fast learner, full of ideas, articulate, bright, witty, trendy, curious, well-informed, flexible

Negative traits: easily distracted, finger in every pie, gossip, superficial, nosy, know-it-all type, internet addict, phone addict, superficial when talking, not always reliable

---

Gemini MC and Leo Rising

Here the communication-focused Gemini meets the flashy Leo. It could suggest the presentation of one's own talent and ideas. It would have a creative edge too, to accommodate the Leo need for creativity. Schools are indicated here too: Gemini for teaching and Leo for its association with the young. Gemini also likes handmade things and Leo is creative (perhaps making gold or orange things or spiritual medals). This is a good combo for business ownership: Leos are owners and Gemini has a flair for sales.

Language and translation agencies would work well here.

Possibilities: Talent Management, Talent Agent, Presenter, Interviewer, Actors, Talent Show Judge, Human Resources, PR Work, Festival Presenters.

Gemini MC and Virgo Rising

Virgo is about craft. Gemini and Virgo in combination need to specialise. They need to identify what they are good at and focus. They have many talents and interests (both are mutable energies) but if they don't specialise in one or two areas, then their energy can be scattered. Lots of famous writers have this MC and AC combination. Both are intellectual energies. They both want to get a message across. They can build a bridge between people: one way might be by building a social media channel.

Gemini loves things to do with the hands and Virgo is about craft, so all kinds of creativity around crafting works here. Virgo is interested in health and healthy lifestyles.

Two mutable energies here are chameleon-like. They can also have two names or two relationships or two different profiles. Gemini is endlessly intellectually curious. They are great at languages.

Possibilities: Writers, TV Presenters, Script Writers, Translators, Sales, Marketing, Language Teachers, Proofreaders, Speech Writers, Journalists, Behavioural Analysts, Song Writers, Astrologers (in ancient astrology, Astrology is ruled by Mercury which also rules Gemini and Virgo. Gemini rules the twilight, things that are hidden, connections between Dark and Light, between the Gods and people. Gemini and Virgo mercurial energies are a bit magical. Astrology works with symbols, which are mercurial too), Bloggers, Independent Operators, Self-made Man or Woman, Health Coach, Candle Making (Virgo: craft, Gemini: twilight and magic).

Cancer Midheaven

Cancer is about protection and nurturing. It is a Water sign and so needs to bond with others. For Cancer MC, there needs to be an emotional dimension to the occupation. Cancer is ruled by the Moon which can represent the mother in the chart. A mother protects and nurtures, feeds, and cares for all your needs. Cancer is one of the parenting signs. They not only care for the needs of others individually but often work for the community, city or nation demonstrating commitment to tribe or place or showing patriotism.

Cancer MC people are personable and excellent at working with the public. But they need to feel they are fully realising their life mission and connecting to their work in a deep emotional way. They need to express their emotionality and their vulnerability.

With Cancer on the MC, the opposite IC sign is Capricorn. Capricorn represents structure, control and the father figure. The parents may have been older than usual or there may have been emotional distance or coldness in the family. Usually there is a powerful authority figure and maybe even indomitable control: "Do this or be this because I say so". This can lead to a tendency to be inflexible and the imperative to stick to a plan or course of action. This can leave the Cancer MC Capricorn IC person stuck in wrong jobs for years. Cancer MCs have a fear of isolation and being judged, especially by their family. It is frightening for them if their family does not approve of their career choice. They need to learn they are not bound by family expectation, or tradition and they should not fear the family's judgment. In the worst scenarios, they feel they can only be themselves once their parents are dead. The best outcome is when they embrace positive Capricorn traits and exhibit these in the supportive 'families of choice' they create.

Cancer MC succeeds in life when they take on a career where they connect to others. Things go wrong for them when they cannot develop their own career and a personally fulfilling achievement. They must embrace their Cardinal mode leadership and 'being in charge' energies. Cancer can be quite private or even shy and need to find a way to demand their own need for status and fulfillment and not just focus on the needs of others.

Cancer MC Traits

Interests: nurturing others, cooking, feeding, home, memories, past, tradition, domestic

Roles: nurturer, chef, property management, domestic worker, feminine role model

Positive traits: domestic, family orientated, caretaker, loyal, sensitive to other's needs, receptive, intuitive.

Negative traits: smothering, moody, living in the past, clingy, co-dependent, insecure, conservative.

Cancer MC and Virgo Rising

Both these signs are concerned with helping. Virgo is about providing a service to others, Cancer about protection and nurturing. Virgo is enthusiastic about health and healthy habits. This could be a good configuration for dieticians and nutritionists or people who advise on weight and diet. Cancer is excited about food: kitchens, hotels, restaurants. Cancer, being a Cardinal energy, needs a position of leadership and recognition. Being a great chef would work here. Virgo likes to deal with knowledge, they are good with gathering and analysing data and compiling spreadsheets. Cancer would be interested in history, so antiquities belong to this combination. Property development belongs here too, because, as well as the Cancer connection to property, there is a need for planning, analysis and the drawing of blueprints, which are all quite Virgoan.

Museums belong to Cancer, so curatorial roles would fit here.

Possibilities: Historian, Chef, Antiques Dealer, Dietician, Naturopath, Childcare, Fitness Instructor, Hotel Concierge, B&B Owner, Nutritionist, Archaeologist, Property Developer, Museum Curator, Archivist.

Cancer MC and Libra Rising

This is the most likely Cancer MC Rising Sign. Libra brings an artistic sensibility and likes to find a harmony of shape, colour and design. Blended with the Cancer orientation to home and property suggests activities like interior design and decoration, renovations and property development again. They work well together towards creating a safe, harmonious and beautiful home. For two cardinal energies, establishing a leading reputation is important. The hotel industry is a fitting arena for this combination. Libra is great at coaching and counselling others, especially helping people weigh their options and make balanced decisions, especially with the personable, emotional connection skills of Cancer in the mix. Libra also excels at diplomacy and can use these skills in conflict management and working towards peace. The legal and judicial skills of Libra combined with the family focus of Cancer would make for good family and divorce lawyers. Both are Cardinal energies and this combination needs to take charge of what they do. Libras are good stylists for others (and being quite vain themselves will always need mirrors around!). In social work, the Cancer MC/Libra AC person will use their skills to weigh and balance the facts (Libra) of a situation and act to protect (Cancer) children or vulnerable people.

Possibilities: Interior Design, Designer, Renovator, Mediator, Visual Artists, Stylists, Spa Work, Feng Shui Consultants, Upholsterer, Beautician, Social Services, Family and Divorce Lawyers or Conflict Management.

Cancer MC and Scorpio Rising

This is one of the rarer combinations. Scorpio is concerned with transformation. Cancer, ruled by the Moon, can talk about the body. So, careers like being gym instructors or dieticians are apt. Transformation (Scorpio) can also apply to the orientation to home (Cancer) for home renovations and re-decoration. Cleansing home of ghosts and entities and negative energy would also be applicable to this combination of qualities. As Cancer can focus on the past and Scorpio is about deep insight, this is a great combination for Past Life Regression work. Both these signs are water signs and both are strongly intuitive. Both signs are interested in emotional connection. A strong Mercury connection (perhaps on the IC) could indicate a talent for mediumship and helping people connect to dead relatives. Family constellation therapy, which involves re-writing negative family programmes that are blocking your development, connects energies of deep insight and transformation (Scorpio) and Family (Cancer). Crisis management and supporting people through trauma and crisis would suit this combination. Water therapies of any kind also fit with this energy.

Possibilities: Dietician, Gym Instructor, Intuitive Therapist, Funeral Director, Energy Clearing of Homes, Exorcist, 'Ghostbuster', Past Life Regression Therapist, Family Constellation Therapy, Surgeon.

Leo Midheaven

Leo requires respect, attention and the status of 'royalty'. Lions are the Kings of the Jungle, after all. They need to become the King or Queen in their work and be regal and dignified. They need a stage and they need to show their accomplishment. Leo is also highly creative, so there should be an element of self-expression. They need to express who they are, without judgement.

Leo MC needs to be respected, admired and wanted. It is disastrous for them to be ignored. A Leo MC usually has a very distinctive appearance that shows their personality, frequently with noticeable 'big' hair: think of a lion's mane. Leo MC fears being overlooked or lost in the crowd. They also fear not being able to contribute something of significance. With a Leo MC, the corresponding and opposite IC is Aquarius. We can look to the ruler of the IC, (Saturn) to give clues as to the blocks a person will encounter on the road to success. The sign and house position of the ruler of MC (Sun) shows the energies you need to express to succeed. The Leo MC needs a degree of showmanship and a chance to entertain. We need to see the Leo personality. There is a strong sense of integrity with Leo, and things will come unravelled if they try to promote a false reputation.

The IC position here is Aquarius. The parents may have been emotionally detached or have tended to treat the Leo MC as a little adult, so they didn't get enough chances to play. There is too much focus on tribe or community and not enough opportunity for our Leo MC / Aquarius IC native to be an individual or 'star'. They have to let themselves take risks, allow themselves to 'be the best', set themselves apart and shine.

A Leo MC usually has a very distinctive appearance that shows their personality, frequently with noticeable 'big' hair: think of a lion's mane. Leo MC fears being overlooked or lost in the crowd. They also fear not being able to contribute something of significance. With a Leo MC, the corresponding and opposite IC is Aquarius. We can look to the ruler of the IC, (Saturn) to give clues as to the blocks a person will encounter on the road to success. The sign and house position of the ruler of MC

(Sun) shows the energies you need to express to succeed. The Leo MC needs a degree of showmanship and a chance to entertain. We need to see the Leo personality. There is a strong sense of integrity with Leo, and things will come unravelled if they try to promote a false reputation. The IC position here is Aquarius. The parents may have been emotionally detached or have tended to treat the Leo MC as a little adult, so they didn't get enough chances to play. There is too much focus on tribe or community and not enough opportunity for our Leo MC/Aquarius IC native to be an individual or 'star'. They have to let themselves take risks, allow themselves to 'be the best', set themselves apart and shine.

Leo MC Traits

Interests: family, people, fashion, associations, stage, fun, risks, themselves
Roles: leadership, speculative businesses, king, queen, diva, centre of attention, shining
Positive traits: generous, confident, charismatic, dramatic, sociable, loyal, loving, and caring, regal, sunny, self-expressive
Negative traits: egoistical, bossy, diva, attention seeker, hungry for praise and attention, proud, self-centred, melodramatic

---

Leo MC and Libra Rising

This is a fairly rare combination of two highly creative and very vain signs. They are both focused on looks, so modelling is a good option for this combination. It is also very strong for visual artists. Libra is about diplomacy and Leo about 'my kingdom' so anything in the realm of public affairs is pertinent. Both signs are very charming and engaging. Libra is to do with partnership and marriage. Leo is about flirtations and love affairs, so careers to do with weddings, like being a civil partnership celebrant or officiant would work here. Both these signs need to showcase their looks and personal confidence. They are highly charismatic and this can be the basis of a certain degree of fame.

Possibilities: Modelling, Visual Artist, Public Affairs Official, TV Presenter, Photographer, Beauty Business Owner, Celebrity Hairdresser, Actors, Business Advisory.

Leo MC and Scorpio Rising

Scorpio is the most common ascendant for a Leo MC. These people are incredibly driven. They strive tirelessly for success and no one should stand in their way. They have extraordinarily powerful charisma; there is a powerful magnetism associated with the Scorpio Ascendant. This is a combination primed for success. There is a conflict in that the Leo MC wants to be flashy and definitely 'seen', whereas Scorpio is more of a reserved and private energy. Scorpio must have a private life. It is a good placement for CEOs and similar senior management roles.

This MC / AC combination can work for achieving the seemingly impossible. Scorpio is a Plutonian and Martian energy. They will fight and dig to get power. Add to this the Leonine drive to be the best and 'on top'. Both are fixed energies, so there is incredible determination and stamina.

Scorpio also has a quality of forensic investigation; they can uncover secrets and what is hidden. Then Leo shines a spotlight on whatever Scorpio has uncovered. Psychological work belongs here, because we are uncovering what is hidden in the mind. Investigative journalism also fits here. The Leo / Sun energy rules football (actually, balls in general), so being a celebrity footballer would work. Politics is a suitable field because it involves power, secrets and the desire to lead and rule.

Scorpio also relates to 'other people's money'. So, investment advisory or stockbroking is a good expression of this combination of qualities.

Possibilities: Politician, Paparazzi, Investigative Journalist, Talent Manager, Psychologist, Actor, Film Director, Professional Footballer (with celebrity status), Stage Hypnotist, Life Coach.

Leo MC and Sagittarius Rising

This is not a common combination. Sagittarius highlights travel here and a career in the travel industry is a strong possibility. Leo needs a stage, of course, and suggests theatrical and drama related work. Sagittarius wants to teach. Sagittarius is related to university and these people might work there or visit universities to make speeches, such as motivational talks. Leo wants to shine and Sagittarius is allied to the Gods, to the divine. So, these two fire energies are really striving to Achieve, with a capital A, in life. Leo likes to know and Sagittarius likes to share knowledge.

Possibilities: University Professor, Holiday Consultant or Representative, Travel Agent, Work on a Cruise Ship, Drama Club, Theatre School, Circus Director, Working with Children (especially on behaviour issues), Racetrack and Horse Racing Betting Activities (Bookies).

Virgo Midheaven

Virgo MC succeeds in a career when they are of service to others and, most importantly, when they *specialise* in something and avoid wandering from job to job. They get into the nitty-gritty details of things. They value being efficient and organised. Virgo MC will have lists, diaries, schedules and records, and this works well for them. As an Earth sign, they must physically manifest their ideas. They must work through their to-do lists, not just dream about them.

They are typically very hardworking (if not *too* hardworking) and highly productive. They are perfectionists. They like to keep control of things.

Virgo is associated with craft and it is important for them to identify and concentrate on building a skill that will be of service to others: service is a key Virgo motivation. They will enjoy becoming a master at their chosen skill. Health, hygiene and healthy habits are common Virgo interests.

Looking at the house and sign placement of Mercury will further refine the ideal career expressions.

A Virgo MC has a natural humility, even in leadership roles. They have a mission to improve the world and bring out the best in themselves and others. One problematic tendency is to be too controlling (Taurus, Virgo and Capricorn can all be control-freaks). They succeed when they learn to go with the flow and be adaptable. They have to guard against being excessively self-critical too.

The Pisces IC identifies the key fear of Virgo MC: they are frightened of chaos and lack of focus. Typically, a Virgo MC gets caught up in the Karpmann psychological 'drama triangle' roles—of victim, saviour or persecutor—in the family of origin, and without insight, can go on to recreate these scenarios in adult life. There is love in their family, but it is confusing, tainted, or over-idealised. Other possibilities are an intensely spiritual family, or one that is socially or physically isolated, or one that is chaotic, perhaps with the presence of destabilising addictions. A Pisces IC child may have been bullied or excluded. They might have felt shy and misunderstood.

The background environment likely lacked appropriate boundaries and The Virgo MC/Pisces IC child learned to be controlling and manipulative to deal with the insecurity they felt. They may have taken refuge in isolation. They need to learn not to deny or control emotion, not to attempt to control others, but to set their own standards and boundaries. It is important not to reject the family because it doesn't meet impossible perfection either. Cutting themselves off from their roots is counter-productive.

They have to take what is best in their family, the idealism, the vision and the love, and incorporate that into a positive expression in their work life in some way.

The Pisces IC can lead to there being dreams and visions with no realistic plan. Virgo MC needs a plan, one that they share with others and continually review and update. To reiterate: they need to specialise and then focus on the plan, systematically and step by step. They fear not being useful to others. When they are of service to others, that is when they are on the path of success. Like all earth signs, they benefit from a connection to the natural world.

Virgo MC Traits

Interests: work, health, data, analyses, lifestyle, herbs, medicine, healing, system

Roles: assistant, critic, trouble-shooter, data analysist, health care worker, PA

Positive traits: a friend in need, reliable, hard-working, clean, organized, prudent, meticulous, wants to be useful, dedicated, unselfish

Negative traits: hypochondriac, pessimistic, overly meticulous, perfectionist, expects the worst, picky, nosy, overly critical

---

Virgo MC and Scorpio Rising

Both of these energies are quite reserved and shy. They will not enjoy the stage or the spotlight particularly. The detailed focus of Virgo works well with Scorpio energy, which is also one of intense research and analysis.

Both signs would like to be seen as intellectuals. The Scorpio energy will need to bond deeply and emotionally with the occupation. They will not be interested in any frivolous activities. They would make good detectives and be well able to analyse evidence. Judges need similar insights (Scorpio) skills and analysis (Virgo). Scorpio is associated with hostage situations and this combination would be good at managing and negotiating hostage situations.

Possibilities: Researcher, Secret Agent, Intelligence Operative, Private Detectives, Police, Judge, Criminal Profilers, Psychologists, Hostage Negotiators.

Virgo MC and Sagittarius Rising

This is a double-mutable combination. It is great for amassing diverse information, then analysing this information and writing books. Writing, books and publishing are good occupations for these two signs. The strong emphasis on communications and knowledge makes a good combination for teachers. Mutable energies can get scattered, so picking a direction and maintaining focus is very important.

Possibilities: Writers, Publishers, Journalists, Reporters, Solicitor or Advocate, Proof-readers, Speech Therapists, Elocution Coaches, Radio and TV Reporters, Columnists, Language Teachers, International Businesses, Analysis of Religions or Cultures, Linguistics.

Virgo MC and Capricorn Rising

It is the blend of energies that suggests an apprentice. This combination wants to keep learning forever. It is a combination that therefore finds it difficult to choose a career. The Capricorn energy wants to climb the ladder of success but the Virgo energy does not have the same ambition so that difference has to be accommodated in the career choice. Capricorn is concerned with hierarchies and traditions. Perhaps a traditional (Capricorn) skill or craft (Virgo) working within a guild or trade organisation would work well. The Virgoan detail-orientation and Capricornian structure make for fine administrators. They are both earth energies and whatever craft or path is chosen, they will need to work steadily to perfect it.

Possibilities: Teacher, Librarian, Medical Personnel or Management, Doctor, Dentist, Teacher of Medicine, Chiropractor.

Libra Midheaven

The Libra MC has a focus on creating balance and harmony. Being air signs, they are interested in connecting with others and they like to work in partnerships. Libra MC would relate to decision making. They would need to be working in a pleasing environment. As a Cardinal energy there is the desire to become a leader and, in such a role, they can inspire others with regard to achieving peace, harmony and balance. Being a Venus ruled sign, the Libra MC is highly artistic. They also have a flair for therapy; perhaps voice or sound therapy (incorporating the orientation to harmony). As the peacemakers of the zodiac, they would excel in negotiation, diplomacy and business, civic or international relations.

The ability to strive for balance and fairness, predisposes them to the legal profession. Being rather vain, they infallibly present themselves in a professional and attractive way and they have pleasing manners and charm to match, communicating well and easily with others. They care about justice, fairness and social issues and would find it rewarding to work towards these things.

They excel in one-to-one situations, like customer service roles for instance, or wherever a partnership of mutual respect can be established. They at best create working environments of peace, harmony and beauty and maintain professional poise at all times. The top qualities are respect, fairness and being law-abiding.

Any personal relationship drama will negatively impact their career success. They have to prepare themselves for successful collaborations-both personally and in business. They also have to find ways to appeal to the public taste.

Fears and pitfalls are indicated by the Aries IC polarity. Something in their background taught them they needed to win at all cost. They were raised to compete, to trust no one and act the lone wolf. Bringing this energy into the workplace can lead to conflict and Libra MC fears conflict. They succeed when they resist self-focus, and learn to 'share the crown'. Above all, they need to avoid playing people off against each other or behaving in passive-aggressive ways. They succeed when they find a way for everyone to win. Although they prefer to have a partner, they have to maintain a balance and be able to say 'No' when they should and not slide into 'people pleasing'. It's about mutual respect and straightforward dealing.

Libra MC Traits

Interests: relationship, being loved and loving others, peacemaker, bridge between people, people pleasing, making things beautiful
Roles: therapists, contractor, beauty industry, mediator, diplomat, law, decorator, networker,
Positive traits: charming, sociable, peace-making, gracious
Negative traits: vain, co-dependent, people pleaser, agreeable, too concerned about their looks and others' looks, hedonistic

Libra MC and Scorpio Rising

This combination would excel at investigating and negotiating relationship issues: Both Scorpio and Libra are concerned with relationships, Scorpio can fathom and investigate the psychological complexities and Libra can assist with resolutions. They could be involved in researching abuses of power (Libra: -justice; Scorpio: dealing with what is what is hidden) at both the personal and the mundane (worldly) level. Both signs make for good therapists. Scorpio rules crisis and transformation and this combination could help people resolve and recover from trauma. The Libran energy is excellent for negotiating and evaluating contracts and Scorpio can speak of joint financial issues, so this combination could be great for financial roles, as bankers or financial loans or insurance advisors. Scorpio is associated with intimacy and this combination can be good for a sex therapist or sexologist.

Possibilities: Chief Justice, Relationship Therapist, Psychologist, Business Contracts Specialist, Make-Up Artists, Advisors on Finance, Loans, and Insurance, Sex Therapist, Performance Management.

[You will notice that several placements and combinations are mentioned as being suitable for therapists. We are not suggesting everyone becomes a therapist; instead that some have talents for understanding people, their motivations and difficulties etc., and can communicate compassionately and can use those qualities in any number of professions. It would be valuable in human resources, line-management roles and performance evaluation, for instance, in the work environment].

Libra Midheaven and Sagittarius Rising

Both these signs are sociable and people-oriented. They are likely to be at the centre of attention. Both are good communicators and are able to bring people together and get people 'on board' with ideas and projects. Sagittarius has a desire to do good in the world and Libra has leadership ability and wants to operate in partnership. With this combination we are uniting the driving principles of Law and Justice. Together they can work to enact legislation or to operate charities, for example.

Possibilities: Union Leader, Lawyer, Judge, Overseas Diplomat, Director of a Charity, Aid Worker, Advocate, Public Relations, Visa Services.

Libra Midheaven and Capricorn Rising

These two energies have very little in common besides their Cardinal modality, which in both cases indicates the need to lead and take charge of something. Libra needs to work in partnership. Capricorn is a driven and capable business-oriented energy, but much more of a lone-operator in enterprises. Libra wants to feel somehow in charge of relationships, achieving this in subtle ways; Capricorn will not enjoy this. So, there is a challenge to find a way for these incompatible energies to co-exist in the career sphere. Libran charm and diplomacy must be used in getting to the highest levels of success and achievement, which is what Capricorn desires. It is the ideal placement for a Self-made Man or Woman. The Libran flair for advising and coaching could be applied in careers such as business advisory and mentoring.

Possibilities: Business Mentorship; Human Resources, Entrepreneur; Life Coach. Lawyer, Judge, Beauty Salon Owner.

Libra MC and Aquarius Rising

This is a very rare combination and produces some very unique people. The idealistic Aquarius energy leads these people to take a moral stand on issues of concern. Libran leadership enables them to lead humanitarian organisations and projects. Work towards equality, perhaps sex and gender equality, would fit here. The Aquarian energy inspires futuristic and innovative projects and methods. Libra MCs tend to be 'people pleasers', Aquarius is about standing for causes and principles. These signs can unite well for charitable aims.

Possibilities: Avant-Garde or Post-Modern Artist, Equal Rights Activist, Charity or NGO Leader.

Scorpio Midheaven

The secretive energy of Scorpio wishes to investigate and penetrate below the surface of things. Being ruled by Mars, they can motivate themselves and get things done. They have powerful gut feelings and intuitively know the right step to take in any given situation. Scorpio is all about power.

Although they need to have their times of solitary retreat to recharge their batteries, they should know that their power is, in truth, inexhaustible.

They are quite inscrutable; they know and hold their secrets. They are unafraid to confront the darker side of life.

What frightens them is to contemplate a life without passion or the experience of betrayal or being lied to. Trust issues are central to them. They want to be loved for themselves, not for money.

They succeed when they follow inner callings and drives. They have investigative and research skills which they may use to expose cheating and lying in the world. They need to be using their sexual magnetism and their intense feeling nature; they have charisma. It is not just sexual magnetism—they can attract the people and the help they need to succeed.

They fail when they get caught up in drama for the sake of it. They can 'eat crisis for breakfast' and this can be compulsive. It is also important to learn that in our new social media world, there are, in a sense, no more secrets.

The Taurus IC shows they were taught to prioritise security and stability. However, they need to be taking some risks to be truly fulfilled and successful; they will have to be accustomed to life on the edge. Something—and this is not necessarily the parents—gave them a strong security base which allowed them to learn rock solid values.

It will be important to use their extraordinary willpower. They have more ability than most to show vulnerability and conquer their fears, including fears of being successful. Scorpio MC must escape their comfort zone and avoid being stuck in the wrong job for decades. The crisis that gets them out of it is the ultimate blessing in disguise. They need to create opportunities and pounce on them. The current transit of Uranus through Taurus is likely to throw up some chances. Being flexible is not going to come easy to someone operating from this fixed sign Scorpio-Taurus axis, but it will benefit them.

They are arch-manipulators, so they should find the most positive way to use that (for example in stock market work). A key Scorpio skill is the ability to transform—both themselves and others; these key partnerships of mutual transformation and empowerment are possible—once they learn to trust sufficiently.

Building a stable home life to retreat to will be an invaluable basis for success out in the world.

Scorpio MC and Sagittarius Ascendant

This is another rarely occurring combination. They might consider some career in which they investigate and analyse ethical issues. They could be insightful and transformative teachers. Scorpio orients to the psychological, Sagittarius to the philosophical. Scorpio is about power and Sagittarius is about analysis and opinion.

Possibilities: Theologist, Archaeologist, Comparative Religious Studies, Explorer of Cultures and Belief Systems, Kinesiologist, Translator or Analyst of Ancient Texts, Specialist in 'Dead' Languages.

Scorpio MC and Capricorn Rising

This is a very dynamic pairing of energies. Both are very ambitious and very driven, work relentlessly for success, and are willing to take calculated risks. Capricorn energy is seeking recognition and Scorpio needs a big financial payoff. There is an impenetrable, emotionally defended quality to this combination. Scorpio rises Phoenix-like from any adversity, Capricorn has staying-power and these energies together make them invincible. They are each tactical and strategic and both Scorpio and Capricorn being quite private energies they are 'not giving anything away'. They need *Respect, Money, and Victory* and are likely to achieve those objectives.

Possibilities: Investment Manager, Politician, Stockbroker, Admiral of the Navy, CEO, Secret Agent, Investigator, MP, Activist for Sexual Political Issues, Writing and Teaching on Strategy and Tactics.

Scorpio MC and Aquarius Rising

There is just a little in common for these two fixed energies. Aquarius is associated with humanitarian concerns and also with technology. The Scorpio emphasis is on power. In the technology field the energies would combine elegantly in development of the newest applications, innovative technologies and progressive web development. Aquarius also rules astrology, and the Scorpio interest in delving into the workings of the mind and uncovering secrets could combine well here for an astrologer. Likewise, for the psychologist or brain scientist, both these energies engage to find ways to understand and optimise how our brains and minds work.

Aquarius is about working towards the betterment of humanity, Scorpio is the master of transformation, so the energies both contribute in activities such as politics, social reform or equality and anti-discriminatory activism.

Both Aquarius and Scorpio energies have the fixity and resistance to change that demands people 'take them as they are'. Aquarius must be uncompromisingly their own person; Scorpio will not trust someone until they have demonstrated their acceptance of them. It will take a while to get to know these people.

Possibilities: App creator, Web Developer, Tech Innovator, Inventor, Scientist, Surgeon, Astrologer, Psychologist, Brain Science and Research.

Sagittarius Midheaven

Sagittarius MC wants to give something back to the universe. It is instinctive (a fire characteristic) and has an adventurous mindset. Sagittarius MC gets bored very quickly and needs to constantly encounter new knowledge. Ideally, they are teaching and communicating what they know and learn. They are born teachers. They learn, think and move fast. As a mutable energy, they may well have more than one career on the go and they frequently undergo at least one major career shift in life.

Freedom is a key factor and they need to always make the choice that promotes personal freedom.

A great career for them could be anything to do with life coaching. They can teach others their knowledge and insights and help people overcome obstacles and instil optimism: Sagittarius rules optimism. They are born motivators.

Sagittarius MC needs to 'think big' and prepare for major success. Modest and small outcomes will not satisfy. What they do needs to be expansive, for themselves and for others. To maximise their finances and self-worth they need a big audience, a world scale, global reach and frequent physical travel.

Their greatest fear is an existence without meaning. They can undermine their success when, concentrating on the big picture, they lose track of details and fail to check the facts and figures. Sagittarius is about 'natural law' and oriented to basic truth, so whatever they do needs to have a strong ethical underpinning if it is going to be a path to success for them.

Gemini on the IC can indicate insecurities around intellect and information. Perhaps they were even told they were stupid. They need to challenge this work to demonstrate their knowledge. They must remember to always get their facts straight and not to undermine themselves by failing to study or prepare thoroughly—no vagueness is allowed! Gemini IC for some reason feels driven to 'out-smart' people and to prove 'them' wrong, the people who doubted their capabilities and cleverness.

It can indicate a family background where they got mixed messages. Sometimes there was a missing family member or the family structure altered at some point.

Having a spiritual outlook and giving back to the world, being generous, will work well for them. They need faith in their knowledge and in themselves. Sagittarius MC is happy once they find their global stage and recognition, at which point they will be able to give their gifts and talents with Jupiterian generosity.

Sagittarius MC Traits

Interests: spirituality, higher learning, divinity, travel, foreign cultures, philosophy, sports, adventure, wisdom

Roles: teacher, guru, spiritual leader, law enforcement, preacher, priest, gambler, publisher

Positive traits: motivator, good communicator, teaching skills, optimistic, having faith, generous, lucky, eternal student

Negative traits: overindulging, greedy, pushing their luck, fanatical, judgmental, preachy, hypocritical, know-it-all

---

Sagittarius MC and Capricorn Rising

There is only a little in common for these two signs. Both are keen on teaching. Sagittarius is the universal teaching sign. Capricorn excels at teaching about the past, for example. So, a good expression for both energies would be being an historian or a history teacher, working with the ancient past. Capricorn rules wisdom, Sagittarius shares knowledge. They can communicate the wisdom of past ages and cultures. This is a great combination for a university professor. Sagittarius also rules legislation, Capricorn symbolises the Judge, so developing and teaching about legislation is a good field. Sagittarius wants to improve the world for humanity. They can be greedy on their own account, certainly, but they always wish for others to succeed, too. Capricorns are a more solitary energy and are motivated to achieve status and recognition; however, they also have rectitude and would not work against others.

Possibilities: University Professor, History Teacher, Judge, Legislator, Archaeologist.

Sagittarius MC and Aquarius Rising

Both these energies have a strong focus on humanitarianism. They want to make the world a better place. It is an idealistic and fair-minded combination. Both are quite adventurous and keen to fight for a cause. Both are concerned with freedom.

One possible expression might be helping refugees, such as handling visa applications. They want to help people become free to live better lives as they desire; to help remove the blocks and obstacles, thus, helping people trapped in addiction and other mental health challenges would work well for this pairing.

Sagittarius has a greedy side; Aquarius has a curious side. Aquarius wants to try everything once; Sagittarius wants to try it again and again. Sagittarius, being a mutable energy, could adapt to almost any path. Aquarius wants to escape traditions and blocks. Sagittarius is about following the divinely ordained path. Aquarius has a political mind, but one oriented to the more breakaway and rebellious interests and radical ideas.

[Note: To distinguish the charity focus of Aquarius and Pisces: Aquarius would represent profit-oriented charities; Pisces non-profit oriented charities.]

Possibilities: Refugee Advocate, Child Protection; Drug Rehabilitation, Charity Organiser, Radical Politics.

Sagittarius MC and Pisces Rising

This combination of energies creates deeply compassionate people who most definitely have their hearts in the right place. They tend to act as saviours. Healing is a Pisces activity; Sagittarian knowledge can contribute in that sphere.

They are not big on the practicalities of life, often drifting into fantasy worlds. If not careful, they only dream of success and do not take the steps to achieve it. Pisces is strongly creative; Sagittarius rules publishing; so, this is an excellent pairing of energies for writers and novelists. Sagittarius can have a tendency to assume they always know best. Pisces can be too dreamy, so might be in need of a wake-up call of some sort to get them to act.

The Piscean side excels at photography, indeed all sorts of visual expression. Costume design would be another appropriate field for them. This MC/AC pair is very good for ceremonies, weddings, celebrations and such. They have somewhat of a taste for the idea of fame and the possibility to achieve that.

They would be good in animal-related careers.

Anything in the spiritual field would suit this combination. Pisces of course wishes to be of service. Sagittarius is the teacher. Together they would excel imparting spiritual values or information about higher realms and compassionate causes.

Possibilities: Teacher, Spiritual Teacher, Guru, Costume Designer, Wildlife Photographer, Travel Writer, Novelist, Animal Handler, Equine Therapy Facilitator.

Capricorn Midheaven

Capricorn is about hard work and perseverance. They are going to get to the end of the tunnel, regardless of the pain they have to experience in doing so. They are aware of the importance of careful planning to achieve success. They work unceasingly, to get recognition and reward. They are stubborn too, and cannot be deterred from their objectives, they will stick to their course. A Capricorn MC is likely to express that they don't want to be like their father; they want to be their own, self-made person and be seen as such.

Capricorn MC succeeds when they accept responsibility and work in a steady, structured way towards their goals. They must become the master at whatever they do and focus on achievement, authority and leaving a legacy.

The corresponding IC is Cancer. These natives fear alienation and criticism from their family circle. For them 'blood is thicker than water' and they are ready to make sacrifices to meet the expectations of others; to honour their heritage, but this can hold them back. They have been taught that family is sacred it and entails obligation and mutual reliance. For this reason, a Capricorn MC often has to leave home to succeed. They have to strike out on their own and take some carefully calculated risks. They find they blossom and grow once beyond the family circle of influence.

Also, a Cancer MC suggests that they would benefit from showing emotion in their work environment. Here, examining the decans, duads, and the sign and house of the MC ruler will be an especially important guide.

They undermine themselves when they do not step up to the positions of authority and leadership they have earned.

Capricorn career possibilities include: Admiral, Politician, Public Defender, Entrepreneur, Employer, Company Start-Ups, Long-Distance Runner, Warehouse Worker, Legal Secretary, Electrician, Business Consultant or IT Manager.

Capricorn MC Traits

Interests: career, accomplishment, business, management, history

Roles: planner, management, leadership, business, supervisor, tester, authority, mentor, professor

Positive traits: hard-working, business-like, serious, realistic, time-management, organised, disciplined, responsible, high standards, cautious

Negative traits: conservative, bossy, stuck in the past, snobbish, sceptical, over-ambitious

Capricorn MC and Aquarius Rising

Although both Saturn ruled, these energies are different. Capricorn is about tradition and the rule of law and is very conservative. Rebellious Aquarius throws away the rulebook and is focused on the future. Both are very independent and both can show great commitment once a suitable path is identified.

Possibilities: Legal Secretary, IT Consultant, Electrician.

Capricorn MC and Pisces Rising

Capricorn MC is focused on structure, discipline and demonstrable achievement. Pisces lives in the world of the intangible and ineffable, dissolves and blurs boundaries and evades all restriction. They will have a challenge to work both of these energies and identify a life path that honours both sensibilities. However, they are brilliantly complementary. A bit of Capricorn structure and discipline can guide Pisces to achievement and help them avoid dreaming their lives away. Pisces gives insight and inspiration to add some warmth, kindness and connection in Saturn's long, hard and often lonely path. Capricorn gives Pisces the framework it needs to use and share their gifts. Pisces teaches Capricorn about forgiveness, compassion and the underlying oneness of all life and experience, even when we feel or operate in seeming isolation; it illuminates the deeper meaning under all Capricorn's portfolio of hard work done and projects realised.

Possibilities: Spiritual or Healing Centre Manager, Chiropractor, Zero Balance, Alexander Technique, Rolfing (and similar joint and skeletal focused therapies), Accreditation and Certification Body Manager for Healing Practitioners, Animal Rescue Centre Manager, Providing Healing in the Corporate World (e.g. lunchtime meditation facilitator; in-house complementary therapies or healing movement classes), Running courses to Heal and Inspire the Work or Business Environment (e.g. Non-violent Communication), Mountain Climber or Mountain Climbing Facilitator.

Capricorn MC and Aries Rising

These are both highly individualistic energies. Both are Cardinal energies with the drive to become leaders. Aries wants to fight the system.

Capricorn wants them to fight the system from within. They have faced hardship and know what goes into getting to the top and they are both here to achieve in this life. This combination never stops pushing and if required will fight against obstacles. The Arian bravery and intuitive drive teamed with Capricorn determination and stamina for the long haul are a combination made for success. Fire and Earth energies are not easy partners, but there are complementary aspects here that will contribute to achievement.

Possibilities: Politicians, Public Defenders, Long Distance Runners, Entrepreneurs, Employers, Company Start-Ups.

Capricorn MC and Taurus Rising

Here we have two earth signs. They need tangible results, security, dependability and to hold onto things financially.

Capricorn again, does not want to be like the father who they don't respect for some reason. Taurus has a focus on self-worth. In fact, both of these sign energies question their self-confidence and ability to achieve, and may have 'father issues' that inhibit them in this way.

Both energies know they have to put the work in. Results may come slowly but they are prepared to crawl, walk, and then run to succeed. They take the time needed to fully understand the environment in which they operate and make careful decisions.

Remember with the Capricorn on the MC, that side is what the world sees; the Taurean traits are the personal motivations.

Possibilities: Bankers, Bank Managers, Investment Managers, Beauty Salon Owners, Property Management, Accountants, Architects, Business Executives, Landscape Architects, Business Owners.

Capricorn MC and Gemini Rising

This combination blends the energies of youth and old age. It is common for these people to achieve something at a surprisingly young age. They are typically 'The youngest person ever to...' or we hear that they 'spoke three languages at the age of six' or something similar.

Capricorn energy wants to invest time and work systematically towards their goal. Gemini is a very different energy; it is eternally curious and always wants to rush off and try something new. These opposing energies can leave the person confused and it will take deep thinking to discover the right thing that they really want to be and do.

One good blending is taking the Gemini talent for communications and becoming a master at it in some way (Capricorn needs to become a master). For example, becoming the best communicator or the best sales person. 'Becoming the best' is a Capricorn thing. Gemini is a natural networker, in the business field they could become a headhunter: finding, communicating and attracting (Gemini) excellence (Capricorn), for instance.

Possibilities: Headhunters, Business Consultants, IT Managers, The Youngest Doctor, The Youngest Teacher.

Aquarius Midheaven

Aquarius MC gives a unique quality and they will tend to be doing something out of the ordinary. Aquarius MC people feel different from others. They don't fit the usual moulds and may be considered 'black sheep'.

An Aquarius MC is never going to be your average representative, whatever the field. They are people that make their own rules. They will abide by others' rules when they see the purpose of them and concur.

They are non-conformists.

This is where you are likely to encounter freelancers and other people engaged in non-typical work patterns and practices.

They have an emotional detachment and go for higher education. They could even be geniuses. Geniuses have to be careful to be objective and treat everyone as an equal. No (Leo IC) superiority is allowed, it will block their best achievement.

Leo IC predisposes them to need to be the cheered and respected leader. Their family might have been one prone to drama, with an aura of entitlement where they expected to be treated as royalty. Not examining and understanding these root experiences can lead to Aquarius MC acting dictatorially and impairing their own success.

It is possible someone in the family of origin was particularly self-centred and loathed to share the spotlight. It is also typical for there to be a missing father figure with a Leo IC. The Aquarius MC influence could have led the individual to 'take refuge' in groups as self-protection.

Aquarius MC succeeds when they ally themselves to principled causes and careers; when they find a niche where they can express their individuality and make innovative contributions to society. They want a humanitarian cause. They fear being misunderstood, ridiculed or excluded for their futuristic ideas. They undermine their effectiveness when they rebel or shock others just for the sake of it.

It is good for Aquarius MC to build a community and unite with their true tribe (which might be an unusual one). They do better if they work with friends, mentors and helpers than they do alone. If the Aquarius MC doesn't feel they belong in a work environment, they are in the wrong one and should move groups.

Aquarius MC succeeds when they embrace and express their individuality, sharing the spotlight and taking care not to create unnecessary drama or upstage others. They need to be conscious always that they are part of the tribe.

Possible careers for Aquarius MC: Professors, scientists; environmental engineers, astrologers, social workers, computer programmers, industrial engineers, toxicologists, activists and reformers.

Aquarius MC Traits

Interests: freedom, groups, friends, computers, technology, trends, modern life

Roles: inventor, computer technician, phone business, innovation, trendsetter, internet related business, scientists

Positive traits: genius, intelligent, unconventional, futuristic way of approach, activists, humanitarian, idealistic, thinking outside of the box, does not want to fit the mould

Negative traits: stubborn, saboteur, rebel, provocative, explosive, erratic, emotionally detached.

Aquarius MC and Taurus Rising

Here is a chart with four fixed angles, so we have a native who wants to hold onto things—to hold on to material things, to hold fast to their principles, to hold on to emotional connections, to hold people's attention and respect.

Taurus wants to build things, often from the ground up. A typical characteristic of a Taurus Rising is to say 'No!', certainly in the first instance. They have to get used to ideas. They are concerned to construct boundaries and protect their own security and comfort, so they are resistant to change.

Aquarius is a fixed energy that also questions, but their concern is about staying close to their principles and their 'truth', so they question the 'truth' of others. Aquarius is interested in social responsibility, and they do need to break some barriers and bring about change, but as a fixed energy, they are slow about it. Both these sign energies are very principled.

Aquarius is unique and Taurus, being Venus ruled, is interested in art and creativity, so this combines well for highly individual artistic expressions.

Taurus is always close to nature, Aquarius fights for important causes, so these energies will unite well for working for environmental protection. Similarly, animal welfare work belongs here and animal rights work.

Taurus has a Venusian connection to love and partnership, so they might also unite with the Aquarian energy to fight for equality in relationships and for different types of relationships.

Possibilities: Environment Activist, Equal Rights Defender, Innovative Artist, Animal Welfare Worker, Animal Rights Activist.

Aquarius MC and Gemini Rising

Both are air signs, all about knowledge and gathering information. Both signs are strongly related to technology also.

These are both outgoing, people-oriented energies. They both want to go out and connect with people. Gemini Rising likes to act as the social butterfly. However, the Aquarian energy is quite detached emotionally in this. The Aquarian interest is in connecting with large groups. Together this combination would be good for YouTube and blog writing. Gemini communicates with ease, and Aquarius has talents, new ideas and genius to share.

They are the world's natural freelancers, needing lots of flexibility and space and the ability to create their own schedules. Both are ideally suited to work with the internet. Aquarius is very keen on the research side (according to their own terms and motivation). There can be an interest in politics, but they might resist being identified with a particular party as they want to express their own unique political outlook.

In whatever field, the Aquarian rebelliousness may surface as they don't want to be forced or ordered to do anything.

Possibilities: Technicians, Receptionists, IT, Bloggers, You-Tuber, Business on Instagram; Psychoanalysis, Astrologer, Scientific Advisor, Authority Figure, Researcher, Flight Attendant (Aquarius- flight), Customer Service.

Aquarius MC and Cancer Rising

Here we are highlighting the protective Cancer energy. Aquarian energy is focused on humanitarian pursuits. These energies are very different. (In the natural zodiac, there is a quincunx between the signs Cancer and Aquarius, and a quincunx is an uncomfortable connection). The challenge is to find a way to blend these dissimilar approaches, so both are expressed.

Aquarius is about innovation: Cancer is about the home. So, one expression might be the new home building technologies, such as pre-fabrication, the phenomenon of tiny homes, etc.

Aquarius is about community and social action; Cancer is concerned with food. It would be a good combination for food banks or other food charities.

Cancer rules women and Aquarius is about community and activism, so this would be good for women's groups and reform organisations, for example rape crisis centres, women's aid, domestic violence shelters etc.

It would also be good for people working for the good of people with special needs.

Possibilities: Foodbank Organiser, Food Aid Charity, Women's Group Worker, Women's Issues Activist, Innovative Housing Initiatives.

Pisces Midheaven

Pisces wants to save others and will sacrifice themselves for a greater cause. They are chameleons who can change and act differently as required in different environments or situations. Sometimes they like to retreat and be alone. They can resort to dramatics on occasion and are highly susceptible to external influences, thus can seem unreliable to others. They can be led and talked into things, not always for their own good.

They are capable of deep spiritual insights and are good at spiritual practice. It will help them to focus on their own divinity and divine power. Work that links them to the divine is ideal.

They are highly intuitive but also tend to be escapist. They fail when they allow addictions to affect them, drugs, alcohol and similar; a mis-directing of their spiritual power into darkness.

Pisces is also the sign of obsession, again Pisces slipping over to the dark side.

They have a clear mission to help others, especially in helping others grow (reflecting their ruler Jupiter). Charitable enterprise is a natural environment for them. They are dedicated to service, but in return need to feel accepted. They must be careful only to be engaging to help those with a true desire to change. The danger is sacrificing themselves in the process or falling into Piscean/psychological drama triangle 'victim—saviour—persecutor' scenarios. These pitfalls are the most likely to undermine success. Boundaries don't come easily to Pisces MC but are essential for success.

Frequent breaks and holidays are very useful for Pisces MC, every three months at a minimum. They need to recharge to be able to effectively help others.

Pisces MC is highly creative and imaginative and should find an outlet for their artistic skills. They can visualise a perfect future, but often are challenged to act on the vision. They need to respect their powerful intuition—it is a super-power and yields essential information for them.

The Virgo IC suggests a family background where parents were excessively critical and demanded an impossible perfection. It leads to a fear of criticism and negativity directed towards them. They might also have been burdened with excessive chores and responsibilities at too young an age.

They can helpfully express their Virgo IC by being well organised at home, giving themselves a good platform of operation from which to achieve their best outcomes.

There is a sense of a highly karmic life experience for Pisces MC people and at some point, in some way, they will be called to embrace forgiveness and acceptance as an empowering strategy in their path to success.

Pisces MC Traits

Interests: music, the arts, alleviating suffering, psychic phenomena, spirituality

Roles: spiritual seeker, dreamer, poet, addict, visionary, dedicated helper, psychic, artist

Positive traits: creative, compassionate, intuitive, imaginative, empathetic, idealistic, spiritual seeker, willing to serve, forgiving, devoted, meditative, non-materialistic

Negative traits: daydreamer, confused, oversensitive, lives in a fantasy world, unrealistic, impractical, addiction-prone, co-dependent, deceitful, unreliable, reclusive, escapist, martyr

---

Pisces MC and Taurus Rising

Here the native will be able to take the amorphous and intangible inspirations available to the Pisces MC and channel them into a concrete and valuable form, be it an artistic expression or something more mundane. The floaty, balloon-like mutable Pisces energy is tethered and grounded by the Taurus Rising. Both signs are highly artistic so it would seem likely that creative activity is a great expression of this combination of traits.

Possibilities: Artist, Poet (perhaps 'concrete poems'!), Singer, Songwriter, Musician, Nature Conservation, Animal Rescue, Dancer.

Pisces MC and Gemini Rising

This is a double mutable combination and as such is suited to working with the gathering and sharing of knowledge. They are very flexible and adaptable. It is quite likely they have more than one occupation at a time.

Pisces needs to be involved with a meaningful cause. Gemini can lend its flair for connection and communication and advance that cause. Pisces is deeply emotional, so the Geminian expression conveys that emotion and it can be compelling to listeners and readers.

Both of these signs are highly creative. Pisces has the inspired imagination, Gemini, the skill to put things into words. Pisces is very visual, so anything involving imagery works for them. It would be great for YouTube and Websites and leaflet design.

It is also an ideal combination for the intuitive readers, psychics, intuitive astrologers and interpreters of dreams. This would be heightened by strong Mercury or Mercury-Pluto placements.

Possibilities: Charity work, Charity Leaflet Handler, Website Developer, Web Design, Songwriter, Paediatrition and Children's Healing, Psychic, Intuitive Reader, Dream Interpreter, Intuitive Astrologer, Puppeteer.

Pisces MC and Cancer Rising

With this pairing we have two deeply caring water signs. There is a strong need to be of service to others. Pisces is concerned with rescuing and saving. Cancer is concerned with security and home. These energies would combine well in building or providing homes to others in need. Cancer can tap into the needs of a community or society and respond to that. Cancer can take the lead and instigate projects. Pisces will be interested in sharing, making, and soliciting donations, and giving their time for a good cause in the interests of others. Pisces MC has the charm and magnetic appeal that could motivate others to give. Both Cancer and Pisces are very nurturing, so caring professions like nursing and medicine belong here. They need to express their empathetic, caring nature.

Past life regression work is an expression of these energies, as is family constellation work, connecting spiritually and healing (Pisces) the past (Cancer). Work to assist refugees would be appealing to these motivations.

This combination will tend to experience plenty of drama in their own family experience.

Possibilities: Nurse, Doctor, Charity Worker, Intuitive Readers, Marine- related Work, Caretakers, Animal Rescue, Family Constellations Therapist, Tarot Reader, Psychics, Healers, Dancer, Herbalist, Mental Health Worker, Refugee Support.

Pisces MC and Leo Rising

Pisces likes the idea of fame and adoration and Leo is very attention seeking. Presenting drama involving creative elements such as photography perhaps would work here. They would excel at making theatre inspired by their own emotional experience, but would want to watch a tendency to create unnecessary spiralling drama around themselves and indulge 'diva' type behaviour; it's a fine line!

Possibilities: Hair Model, Actor, Wedding Organiser, Photographer, Celebrity, Services to Celebrities, Beauty and Make-Up Artist, Model, Fashion Design, Drama Circle or Drama Club Organiser.

Working with Essential Dignity

When we are looking at a birth chart, for vocational or other analyses, we need to determine the relative importance of the different planetary players. By looking at essential dignities we get an indication of the strength of the ruling planet of the chart and of each house. Essential dignity is not the preserve of horary analysis, it is invaluable for understanding natal charts too. We systematically assess all the factors contributing to planetary strength, as detailed on an essential dignities table or report for the birth chart. Here is your condensed guide to using the essential dignities.

First determine whether planets are in rulership, exaltation, fall or detriment to determine the strength: Rulership 100% Exaltation 80% Triplicity 50% Term 30% and Face 20%. A planet in rulership is 'the King'; a planet in exaltation is 'the Guest of the King', reflecting status.

Triplicity relates to the elemental nature of signs. Signs have triplicity rulership depending on whether it is a day or night chart:

Fire signs are ruled by the Sun in the day and Jupiter at night. Earth signs are ruled by Venus in the day and the Moon at night. Air signs are ruled by Saturn in the day and Mercury at night.

Water signs are ruled by Mars both in the day and the night.

Planets in angular houses (1,4,7,10) have the most effect; succedent houses (2, 5, 8, 11) less so; cadent houses (3,6,9,12) positions indicate the planet 'falling from power'.

Relative strengths of houses: Angular planets have 100% strength; Succedent 50%; Cadent 25%.

Consider that malefics in weaker houses are diminished in ill effect. If you have a weak planet in a strong house, there will be troubles to experience, but you can take action to alleviate the situation.

Houses 6, 8 and 12 are 'dark' houses and can indicate highly karmic or strong psychological issues.

Cadent houses are for visionary thinkers, not such active people. If a cadent house planet is related to a blockage, it will tend to be a mental blockage rather than a challenging event. The order of strength of the most active houses are: 1, 10, 7, 4, 11 and 5.

Positions of rulership or exaltation for highly functional planets contribute to an easier path to success, whereas detriment and fall positions suggest there is something to be overcome.

Exalted planets experience ups and downs in strength; it is not a reliable or persistent influence.

Aspects to the MC modify the expression. Find the three closest aspects to the MC within ☌3, then choose the strongest planet to be your career indicator.

Retrogradation will reduce the strength of a planet and delay success but not negate it.

A peregrine planet has no essential dignity, no strength at all, and is described as 'the exiled or homeless one'.

Unaspected planets are termed 'feral'.

Planets are not good or bad, there are just some that need more work to make them successful.

House position and other factors impact the essential dignity or strength of a planet thus:

Factor	Points
In 1st or 10th house	+5
In 7th 4th or 11th house	+4
In the 2nd or 5th house	+3
In the 9th house	+2
In the 3rd house	+1
Direct (not retrograde)	+4
Swift of motion	+2

Factor	Points
Saturn, Mars or Jupiter oriental (clockwise from the Sun)	+2
Mercury or Venus occidental (anticlockwise from Sun)	+2
Waxing Moon	+2
Free of combustion	+2
Cazimi	+6
Partile conjunction with Venus or Jupiter	+5
Partile conjunction with the North Node	+4
Partile trine with Venus or Jupiter	+3
Partile sextile with Venus or Jupiter	+3
Conjunction with Regulus 29° Leo	+6
Conjunction with Spica 23° Libra	+5
Trine or Sextile the Part of Fortune	+5

Swiftness of motion describes whether a planet is travelling at more or less than its average speed:

Average speeds in degrees per day are:

Sun	0.59
Moon	13.11
Mercury	0.59
Venus	0.59
Mars	0.31
Jupiter	0.05
Saturn	0.02

We score for all factors, adding the points

Any planet with more than 17 points is very strong, so would be a good career planet.

As well as essential dignities, there are 'accidental dignities':

Accidental dignity	Points
In the 12th	-5
In the 8th or 6th house	-2
Retrograde	-5
Slow	-2
Saturn Jupiter or Mars occidental	-2
Mercury or Venus Oriental	-2
Conjunct Algol 26° Taurus	-6

We might also consider if a planet is out of bounds. There are no points accorded to critical degrees.

We add the points of all natal planets and use the strongest planet as a career planet.

Mutual receptions and 'mutual deceptions' also have an impact.

This is positive if two planets in each other's signs by rulership or exaltation are friendly to each other, if they have similar natures. Enemy planets in each other's signs by rulership of exaltation have a negative impact on strength.

Friendly planets are:

Moon and Venus	+6
Saturn and Mercury	+6
Sun and Mars	+6
Jupiter and any planet except Mercury	+6

Enemy planets:

Venus and Mars	-3
Moon and Saturn	-3
Sun and Saturn	-3
Jupiter and Mercury	-3

A very positive mutual reception should be factored into career analysis. Find an opportunity to express this connection.

Using essential dignity information will help you choose the strongest planet as your key career planet.

The MC Ruler

The next thing to investigate building your Midheaven profile is to explore the nature of the ruler of the MC. We need to determine the sign, element, modality and house position of the ruler, its relative strength (using the essential dignities table) and any aspects it makes.

MC Ruler in the First House

These people are self-starters and they are out to make a name for themselves. They work very hard and they trust their instincts, as well as need to either use their body or their charm in their work—he sign will suggest which. Quite often they will wear a uniform (nurse, nun, military, etcetera). If the ruler is really close to the ascendant it can bring fame, depending on the strength of the planet. It can also correlate with politics, especially in Scorpio or Capricorn. It is essential to 'put themselves out there', not to hide away. They need to always follow their gut instincts.

Examples: Sagittarius—Pioneer; Fire Signs—Entrepreneurs; Fire—Athletes; Water—Water sports; Capricorn—Construction; Scorpio—Police

MC Ruler in the Second House

These people need to express their personal values in the work they do. They need to consider self-worth, what inspires them, and makes them feel worthy. They need stability in their work situation and feel personally secure with a secure job.

Money is significant to them. It might contribute to self-worth or they might work in finance. They should ask themselves, "Do I judge mine and others' worth by the amount of money they have?"

As they hold onto things, storage is a resonant idea. A storage company would be appropriate, as would security work. Anything sourced from the earth is a suitable occupation.

Their work needs to be concrete and provide a livelihood, possessions, and money. On a psychological level it should be of real value and boost their self-esteem. On a spiritual level it should reflect their ability to manifest things, and mirror their relationship to desires, attachments, and how they show generosity, their offerings to the world: learning to be more generous is key.

Ancient astrologers cast this position as the 'road to Hell' reflecting beliefs in the dehumanising effects of contact with money. A lesson is to let go of material and physical attachments, not be a hoarder or a miser and turn more to spirituality. This is tough for Scorpio and Pisces especially.

Examples of suitable work: Banking, Real Estate, Product Management, Auctions, Food Industries, Farming, Architecture, Designing gardens, Landscaping, Cosmetics, Beauty, Finance, Economics, Sales, Trade, Singing, Voice-Overs, Biology, Interior Design (especially with Libra), Luxury goods.

MC Ruler in the Third House

To find success these people need to use their ability to communicate: Writing, speaking, sign language, etcetera. Writing is associated with mute signs (the water signs are the mute signs; the loud signs are air signs and would suggest speaking roles).

They should explore how they relate to people. They should be using logic, rationality, curiosity and intellect and be always refreshing their knowledge. Air and fire signs particularly will gravitate to fast-paced environments. They can multitask and need to switch between activities.

They are ready to make shifts in their thinking. It can be key to resolve issues with siblings, perhaps karmic issues.

Suitable work includes: Technology, Social Media, Web-based work, Journalism, Writing, Speaking, Profiling, Investigation, Talk Show hosting, Engineer (the type depends on the sign), Advertising, PR, Marketing, Transport, Cars, Agencies, Teaching, Hosting courses). The key is to link the sign to the third house.

MC Ruler in the Fourth House

There is a relation to the family here, or possibly a need for emotional closeness in the work. Home-based businesses and family businesses would relate to a fourth house MC ruler, as does Real Estate. Examples are: with Gemini—selling houses, with Pisces—'saving' families, as in social work.

There will be a need to ensure they balance home and work life.

IC blockages are in play here. They may be impacted by family conditioning, for example thinking they don't deserve success.

Suitable careers: Landscaping, Agriculture, Farming, Air BnB, Renting-with regular payment (especially with a sixth house connection), Buying and selling houses (especially with an eighth house connection), House sales agent (third house connection), Agencies in general (ninth house connection), Funerals or connecting with ancestors (Scorpio on the cusp), Things relating to emotional wellbeing (with water or earth signs, they might support others), Hotels ('temporary homes'), Antique furniture (with Capricorn), Cleaning services (with Virgo), Psychology (with Scorpio) Submarines, seas and oceans- being at the bottom of the chart (with Pisces), Growing herbs (with Virgo), Growing cannabis (with Scorpio), Cooking (with Taurus) Museums (Sagittarius/ Capricorn), Animals (Virgo), Advertising (with 9th house, Jupiter and Moon).

MC Ruler in the Fifth House

These people need a job which is fun. They need to ask themselves how do I express myself and am I ready to shine? If there is a water sign on the cusp it is quite a psychological house, they need to develop their inner self. These people can create atmospheres and can be nurturing- they respond to people's moods. There is also a need to take some risks, so self-employment might be suitable.

The fifth house can be a career indicator in any chart. The sign on the cusp determines how it will express itself. The fifth also reflects money made from the fourth house, for example with an aspect between the rulers of the fourth and the fifth there might be potential to make money from property. The fifth does relate to gains.

Career ideas are: Things to do with the stage and acting, 'Following their heart', Working with children, Making people feel good, Having fun, Using your personal expression and creativity, Sweets, Making children's toys (especially with Jupiter- fun toys are the fifth, teaching toys are the sixth) Toy Stall or Shop, With Sagittarius influence they must aim high-possibly teaching, Entrepreneurs, Cardiologists, Working with gold, Jeweller, Spokesperson, Hairstylist.

MC Ruler in the Sixth House

These people are very hard working. They need to specialise and then focus strongly on achieving professional excellence. Organisational skills, good administration, planning, and efficiency habits serve them well. They have the talent and the ability to see things through to success. Typically, they don't want to become bosses, rather the boss's right hand man. With a Capricorn influence they might aspire to managerial roles, but only reach CEO level with something like a supportive trine from the ruler to the MC.

Suitable work includes: Admin and Payroll, all health fields, Statisticians, Archivists, Systems Analysis, Auditors, Hygiene Inspectors, Nutritionists.

The sixth is the second from the fifth, so possibly they work at what they have fun doing (especially if fourth and fifth house rulers are conjunct) or work with dating websites (especially with an Aquarius influence).

MC Ruler in the Seventh House

These natives need to deal in partnership in the work situation. They will have to use diplomacy and negotiating skills to succeed. They will do well working to create community. They have to show others their skills and abilities and can excel helping others to develop their gifts. Consultancy is a suitable type of work for them. In general, anything that depends on grace, style, beauty and harmony is ideal.

The MC ruler describes the character you need to embrace for a best path to success. It gives you a toolbox of qualities to demonstrate.

Working with a partner at work or personal partner works well for the MC ruler in the 7th house. They are brilliant at customer service and people-facing roles. If there is a stellium in the seventh, it suggests that feedback is vital, feedback for them and for others. As the seventh is the house of competitors and enemies, they might benefit from competition and thrive by being tactical.

Suitable career path: Lawyer, Judge (with Saturn or Sagittarius influence), Attorney, Dealer, Beauty industry, Graphic design (with an earth sign), HR (with air or water influences), Diplomacy (with Sagittarius), Marketing, Advertising, Counselling, Telemarketing.

MC Ruler in the Eighth House

This house placement for the ruler gives individuals who can investigate, research and dig deep. They can plumb the psychology, mindsets and motivations of others. They can be distracted by strong emotions, but shouldn't reign in desires too much, it would stifle them.

The eighth house relates to shared finance, so banking is applicable or possibly the stock market especially with a link to the fifth. There is a link to sexuality so anything in the sex industry is a possibility. The death industry is an eight house area. Occultism can interest these people (the eighth and the ninth relate to the occult, the eighth to the more psychological fields). They will have to safeguard their own psychic energy. Evolutionary and psychological astrology would work too.

As the house of joint resources, working with others can work well for them. In general, they are motivated by the need for power. They can 'eat crisis for breakfast' so crisis management is a good field (especially with Aries, Leo or Scorpio). Managing natural disasters such as earthquakes might apply if there is a Uranian influence.

Possible work fields: Psychologist, Police, Crime, Forensics, PI, Sex Worker, Sex Therapist, Funeral Director, Mortician, Tarot Reader.

MC Ruler in the Ninth House

These people are natural teachers. (The third house collects data, the ninth shares knowledge). They are also attracted to the spiritual, so they benefit from work connected to divine power or the gods, including religious occupations. Communicating divine messages or working with past lives are possible.

Anything connected overseas and foreign topics relates to the ninth house.

If they search for the meaning of life for too long, life passes them by. They can be overly optimistic. They tend to be either rebellious against education or very keen to pursue a degree.

They have a strong moral code and a commitment to truth, so the legal field can inspire them.

Suitable career paths: Tour guides, Travel-related occupations, Dog Sitters, Aircrew or Pilots, Aviators, University Professors, Publishers, Religious occupations (especially with Pisces), Visa work, Supreme Court work, Import and Export.

MC Ruler in the Tenth House

These people are driven to achieve, to take charge and to rise to the top. They are prepared to climb the ladder and relate to authority well, just as well, as their career will depend on their bosses. They want to be respected.

They succeed by being professional and organised at all times and following a structured career pathway. The MC describes the path they need to follow and the qualities they need to portray for all of life, including finances, to optimise their experiences. They also benefit from having good assistants.

Typical career choices: Politics, Local Councils, Business, Business Owners, Accounting, Management.

MC Ruler in the Eleventh House

The toolbox for people with this MC ruler placement includes good teamwork and using networking skills. They are essentially humanitarian. They have an attitude of equality, not seeing themselves as above anyone. If they are leaders, they see themselves as part of a team focused on the same goal. They have the ability to spot significant trends and have the capacity to change and adapt to changing circumstances.

In the eleventh house, you 'make your own family': fans, social media followers, etcetera. It is a very lucky, 'fairy godmother' type house, so expect good luck and surprises.

Typical work areas: Internet, YouTube, Activism, Advisory, Agency, Clubs, Organisations, Invention, Astrology, Weather Forecaster.

MC Ruler in the Twelfth House

Traditional astrology considered the twelfth house a workhouse. As the 'cosmic womb' it indicated the karmic resonances you carried into this life and information on the reason you were born. Also, being in sextile to the MC is an indicated opportunity that might arise for career.

Although a 'dark house' the twelfth house is not all bad news. It does show there will be psychological issues to overcome. The key thing is that when setbacks occur, the individuals should strive to pick themselves up and carry on as soon as possible. Twelfth house and eighth house issues can be places people are prone to wallow. People with this placement can be either exceptionally good or exceptionally bad at manifesting visions. There can also be financial issues to deal with.

There might be something hidden about their work: hidden costs, hidden income, undeclared income.

It is a spiritually inclined placement, so retreats, dream interpretation and similar are their strengths. They need to connect to higher powers or work with 'the unseen'. Not-for-profit charities are suitable arenas for them too, so perhaps working with those struggling with addiction could be a good option. They can work in secluded places like monasteries, hospitals and prisons (but are essentially 'in their own prison' in some sense).

Suitable work choices might be: Past life regression, Inner child work, Shamanism, Bartending, Film-making, Marine occupations, Photography, Social Work.

Planets Aspecting
on the Midheaven

Important information is yielded by the planet which makes the closest aspect to the Midheaven.

In considering planets in aspect to the Midheaven, we use a 10-degree orb, a relatively wide orb reflecting the power of this angle. We consider the five main Ptolemaic aspects:

Conjunctions, Squares, Oppositions, Trines and Sextiles

Conjunctions: A planet on the MC becomes a career or professional planet. What it does is take over the sign, the modality and usually the rulership of the MC and change the expression. We tend to feel that planetary influence more than other factors. It can be positive or negative in influence. Following that planetary influence can work out for people, sometimes. Planets on the AC act similarly, and as the AC is a decision point, it hugely impacts career.

A conjunction has a solar energy. If we merge the planetary energy with the MC, we create success, and not doing so results in failure. Conjunctions can be related to the ninth house—the Sun 'joys' in the ninth house.

Oppositions: Planets in opposition to the MC (i.e., on the IC) relate to heritage and how we use the planetary energy in our family life. With a planet on the IC, there is something you have to embrace about your family life or roots in order to reach success. Some aspect of the opposing planet will block your progress otherwise. Often this indicates a person blocking your success; a partner, child, or other family member.

Oppositions tend to be very challenging aspects, and are hard to reconcile.

The quality of an opposition is Saturnine. So, in a Saturnine way, our experience of an opposing planetary energy gets better with age. Saturn is the furthest of the traditional planets from the Sun and this reflects the 'distance we must travel' and the difficulty we will have integrating the energy.

An opposition is said to have a twelfth house quality. Saturn 'joys' in the twelfth, the house of 'inner demons'.

Squares: These planets at 90 degrees to the MC motivate us and ultimately can 'fix' our reputations as we bring that planetary energy into alignment. It indicates challenges too, but these are challenges with important opportunities embedded in them. The square aspect shows an energy we absolutely have to work with, altering our behaviours and attitudes with respect to that influence in order to unlock its money-making/success potential. There is tension around this planet and the issues it throws up for us. Squares have the quality of Mars (combative, challenging, motivating, energising).

The square has a 6th house energy. Mars 'joys' in the sixth—there is an association with lifestyle choices and the things you can do to fix issues and smooth the way.

For example, with Venus in square to the MC there are possibly issues around self-worth. Do you not believe in yourself and your talent? Do you think you are not beautiful enough? Or perhaps the issue is money: do you not have enough money to proceed?

There is often less of a problem from a square than an opposition or conjunction. We experience it as a push to do something, as a 'kick in the butt'. It is a catalyst, a jumpstart that impels us to action.

Trines and sextiles: These harmonious aspects are going to clearly show job opportunities that will work in harmony with the divinely-inspired mission indicated by the MC.

Trines: Trines to the MC can indicate natural talents and money-making possibilities. Trines have a Jupiterian energy, they show ways to find abundance, including possible sources of income, but definitely leading to personal growth. The trine suggests abundance, but also greed and laziness. Too many trines and free-flowing energies are hard to work with, so we should be grateful for our squares for giving us the impetus to grow and evolve. It calls for 'teamwork' between the two planets or planetary energies involved in the trine. The talents may seem so natural to us that we do not even recognise them as talents.

Trines to the MC present themselves as opportunities, but paradoxically it can be harder to deal with than a square. It does not present as a problem that captures our attention and we may fail to see the opportunity.

Trines have an 11th house quality. It is the house of dreams and wishes—but only if you act upon them.

Sextiles: indicate talents and also choice. Sextiles are a Venusian energy, so you are going to have the *choice* to develop the talent indicated. A Venus placement in your chart does indicate potential sources of money too. Sextiles have a playful quality. Any planet sextiling the Midheaven shows a talent that can earn money. Work out what the aspecting planet, in its particular sign position and house position could symbolise. If you put energy into the sextile energy it will give success, whatever the planet it is.

Sextiles have 5th house quality; the 5th house is where Venus 'joys' and this reflects the playful energy of sextiles.

For example: Suppose there is a sextile to Mercury in the twelfth house in Capricorn. Mercury could relate to astrology (Mercury is the traditional significator of astrology), as well as to communication in general. The twelfth house can relate to secretiveness. Capricorn speaks about leadership. One possibility could be a role looking into people's hidden motivations in order to guide them to career success. Or one might manage (Capricorn) teaching of reading and writing skills (Mercury) in a prison (typical twelfth house environment).

In considering planets aspecting the MC, focus to begin with primarily on trines and sextiles: these talents to be brought out and expressed. Squares and Oppositions are the secondary consideration; these are characteristics that need to be considered.

Remember for any aspect to consider, check if the planets 'get along', i.g., Saturn and Moon are inimical.

Outer planets

We do not experience the outer planets as we do experience the traditional seven planets. We do not experience their full cycles with respect to our birth charts in a human lifespan: at best we experience a Uranus square, Pluto spends 32 years in the sign of Taurus alone. The outer planets are more descriptive of collective energies and generational influences. They typically have psychological rather than material impacts.

Orbs

Orbs are the 'sphere of influence' of a planet. The MC is a 'fictional' point: there is nothing actually there. The MC has a solar quality, but unlike the Sun radiates no light. For that reason, the orbs we accord in defining MC aspects are very strict.

Traditional orbs are:

Planets	Orbs
Sun	17°
Moon	12°
Mercury	7°
Venus	7°
Mars	7°
Jupiter	9°
Lunar nodes	4.5°
Black Moon Lilith	2°
Major Asteroids	2°
Fixed stars	2°
Minor asteroids	1°
Chiron	3.5°
Part of Fortune	2°

MC doesn't exactly have an orb, but we allow 10°.

To determine whether two points or planets are in aspect, we add together their allowable orb and divide by two.

Hellenistic and traditional teachings suggest that any planet within three degrees of the MC must be factored into analysis, especially when we are considering vocation.

Asteroids could be considered as well as planets, but only if within one degree of exactitude in their aspect to the MC.

Retrogradation of the aspecting planet doesn't affect the influence much, just that the energies are more internalised.

I don't consider conjunctions where the planet is in another sign than the MC, or other 'out of sign' aspects, but you can if that is your preference.

A connection to the Ruler of the MC is significant too, but different. The planet conjunct the MC suggests a particular direction of activity. A planet conjunct the Lord of the MC could be considered a money-making indicator; a powerful aspect, but is not quite the same.

Sun on the Midheaven

This is a great conjunction to have. It does not absolutely guarantee success but the Sun does want to shine, it wants to be the best. With the Sun here, the native wants to achieve this on their own. The Sun demands recognition and Sun MC people need to be noticed and respected for what they do. They want to be someone people look up to.

With the Sun at the Midheaven there is often a need for solitude and therefore experience some loneliness, but solitude is necessary to achieve the goals.

These people have often felt weighed down by parental expectations, most probably from the father. They need to be in control of their own lives and in some cases will rebel strongly against this overbearing influence. In a business they need to be able to run the business for themselves. There is a tendency to believe they know better than anyone, but the more rebellious they are, the less successful they are.

People with the Sun on the MC are impossible to ignore, they have a really strong presence. They have a natural confidence and attitude that inspires trust, so tend to end up in positions of charge and executive control.

Solar career choices include: Entertainment, Sport, Speculative Venture, CEO, Business Ownership Jeweller, Goldsmith, Cardiologist, Hairstylist, Director.

Suppose you had Sun on the MC in Cancer, with the ruler of Cancer (the Moon) in Sagittarius conjunct to Uranus in the third house. The Sun rules goals, the head, things that shine and gold, for example. A Cancer MC could speak of protective instincts, children, nursery schools, food, leadership and intuition. Moon in Sagittarius can suggest a 'High Priestess' energy and an interest in spirituality (possibly astrology, too, given the conjunction with Uranus). Uranus also indicates something unique or futuristic. Sagittarius is concerned about 'natural' justice and is benevolent, perhaps the desire to stand up for others. The third house can speak about teaching and writing. Sagittarius rules publishing. The Sun wants to be looked up to and admired, but here it must achieve this in a Cancerian way. So possibly the native could be admired for nurturing and protecting, perhaps by teaching (Sagittarius) children (Cancer) to read and write (third house) in a Primary School (third house). In this way the various energies must be blended to suggest optimal career paths. Then it is necessary to check whether the possible career would be palatable to the Rising Sign, and adjust as necessary. Another possibility could be: Owning and running (Cardinal MC) an esoteric (Sagittarius Moon) cake shop (Cancer MC and Sun) with books (third house Moon).

Moon on the Midheaven

Moon on the MC is all about intuition and the importance of developing and using your intuition. The Moon can also be the sign of a teacher. There can be a need to preach in some way, especially if the MC and Moon are in the ninth house.

The Moon signifies the body, so Moon at the MC can indicate healing and health-related occupations, if not using the body very directly as part of your career success path, for example modelling, dancing or massage.

Moon is ruler of Cancer and thus associated with the fourth house, so speaks of all things related to home, land and property. One expression of this might be work to do with real estate.

A significant quality of the Moon is its fluctuating nature. The Moon waxes and wanes and regulates the tides that rise and fall in the ocean. It is allied to emotion and therefore mood, which changes continually. So, in choosing or understanding your path you will want to accommodate these 'waves' of motivation, energy and activity. This 'to and fro' nature might elegantly describe the comings and goings of an import-export business (for a Moon in Sagittarius, perhaps?).

For the Moon especially, the sign position is highly significant. Moon at the Midheaven is very happy in Cancer or Taurus, and fairly happy in Pisces, too. In Scorpio, Virgo or Capricorn the Moon is not very happy at all. If you have one of these 'depressed' Moon signs at your Midheaven, perhaps it is not the best idea to use your Moon on the MC as your lunar indicator for a suitable career. However, any trines or sextiles to this planet remain valid and useful indicators of talents and opportunity open to you. With good aspects to the MC and a debilitated Moon you can overcome the issues presented; with challenging aspects the outlook is less good. Often with the problematic Moon sign position here, as the Moon is a mother archetype, this could suggest that a difficult relationship with the Mother can impact the native and influence their worldly success. Perhaps the native is trying to 'step into their mother's shoes' or the mother has imposed her ideas and beliefs to the extent that the person doubts their own instinct and intuitions that might be contrary. With the Moon in this position the key is always to tune into and trust your intuition and gut feelings.

As we mentioned, Moon on the MC often denotes a healing path. In order to successfully fulfil a success path as a healer, the MC Moon native must first address any mother issues. The Moon sign is your guide: For example, an Aquarius Moon can indicate a mother who is distant or absent; a Capricorn Moon a mother who is emotionally rigid; a Virgo Moon a Mother who is constantly scrutinising; Taurus Moon, a mother who overfeeds. Any issues like this can impact your vocational success.

Moon is a highly creative energy. Ancient astrology gave the rulership of writing to the Moon, most especially writing about feeling and emotion. So, Moon at the MC can be the signature of poets and novelists.

Anything to do with the oceans, seas, rivers and waters of the world belong to the Moon. Fluids in general are in this domain.

Lunar MC career choices include: Maritime professions (e.g., Fishing, Oceanographers, The Navy), Body-related work, Healthcare, Caring roles, Antiquities and Museums, Hospitality, Restaurants, Alcohol or Drug-related occupations, Real Estate, Social Work, Coaching and Life Coaching, Biologists, or occupations where you work at home.

Chiron on the MC also relates to healing. As it is the Wounded healer archetype this suggests that your own healing path is central to the development of your own healing gifts.

Mars on the Midheaven

Mars is a pioneering and provocative energy. Mars on the MC is good at getting others to stand up for them and at standing up for others. Mars is good at fighting for a cause, and typically fights for their own survival.

There may be family experiences of violence, so they either learned to fight or to abhor fighting. Mars MC energy is good at enforcement and reinforcing: policing/law enforcement, for example, or reinforcing legislation. They are a start-up type of energy. Mars rules logic, so it looks for things that will logically make money. There is an aptitude for sport and for engineering. In other epochs, they could have been professional hunters.

Always check the houses that Mars rules. Mars ruling the seventh house points to success through relationships; Mars ruling the second house indicates fighting or standing up for my own money, possibly working in banking. The house placement of the ruler of Mars is very important here because the profession might well belong to that house.

Possible Mars-related careers include: Hunting, Pioneering, Entrepreneurship, Personal Trainer, Military roles, Police, Sports, Mechanics, Engineering, Manufacturing and Welding.

Venus on the Midheaven

With Venus on the MC your warmth, personal charm, gracious manners and pleasing appearance will appeal to people and be helpful to you in your work. Venus is about harmony. With this placement you are able to have a soothing effect on your work environment. You do well in environments with plenty of empathy and connection going on—these are characteristics suiting the Libran side of Venus.

As for the Taurus side, that is good for planning. Taurus is always comparing things and looking for deals. The Taurus is not stingy, they will spend money, but only for real quality, comfort and value. Libra will be more liberal spenders and seduced by fashionable labels.

Being about connection and relationships, Venus on the MC could point to lucky breaks in career through 'who you know'.

The Venusian energy on the MC is good for career choices like Banking, Finance, Real Estate, Interior Design, Stylists, Economists, Fashion Industry, Artists, Therapies, any type of Consulting, Modelling, Gardeners, Hairdressers, Wedding or Event Planners, Matchmakers, Tailors, Landscape Designers, Graphic Designers, Advertising, PR or HR, Referees and Mediators, Architects.

Remember again to look at the house that Venus rules and the sign of the MC.

Say for example Venus is in the fifth house: This could suggest that money is coming from your own creativity or through some sort of stage or platform.

Say the MC is in Cancer: does this at first glance suggest banking? Not really, because Cancer is more about care and nurture. Fashion, Tailoring and Gardening all suit, being things you can do at home. However, if it happens that Venus rules the Eighth house, then perhaps Finance could be reconsidered, but you would want to find a Cancerian way of doing it.

Perhaps advising people on Personal Finance and Mortgages, as the personal connection and real estate aspects speak to the Cancerian energy.

[Actually, this configuration might also indicate inheriting money from the mother.]

Mercury on the Midheaven

Mercury is excited by gathering and sharing information. They can be gossipers, so be careful about confiding secrets to people with Mercury on the MC. They are the original salesmen who could "sell ice cubes to Eskimos." They are unendingly curious to learn new things and they can talk to anyone about anything.

They excel in areas to do with communications like writing, speaking, telecommunications, marketing and working with the internet. Mercury rules the hands as well as writing, so gaining a craft skill like carpentry or being a silversmith are other expressions.

You need to check the houses that Mercury rules for a more detailed direction. These people are versatile and adaptable, so they will find many possible outlets.

When they have chosen a path, they have a gift for promotion that can serve themselves and others.

Mercurial career choices (naturally a long list) include: Astrology (Mercury was the traditional signature for Astrology), Communications, Business, Writing, Marketing, Sales, Promotion (self and others), Internet, Telecommunications, Media, PR, Languages, Teaching, Postal Services, Trading, Speakers, Medical Professions, Healthcare, Dieticians, Administrators.

Jupiter on the Midheaven

Jupiter can be involved in several different career areas. Law is probably the strongest association, given the highest expression of Jupiterian energy is associated with Justice, the higher good and benevolence. Jupiter in its most elevated expression wants everyone to receive life's bounty, wealth and goodness and for everyone to be free of restrictions (in a way 'free of Saturn'). However, what usually brings best results in life is a balance of Saturnian and Jupiterian influence.

Jupiter is also associated with wealth, but not just money. It is about charity, generosity, giving and kindness. It is a 'Santa Claus' sort of energy, abundant, jovial and humorous ('Ho, Ho, Ho').

Jupiter is concerned with the principle of law ('natural law' and justice). Saturn is concerned with the practical execution of law (and 'the rules'). If you consider the analogy of traffic lights: Saturn describes the traffic regulations and the practical timing of the lights, Jupiter describes the 'higher principle' of saving lives and co-operating for the wider good.

Jupiter MC people love to teach and are naturally suited to anything that has a global reach and involves travel, foreign cultures or broadening horizons in general.

Jupiter is associated with anything that contributes to hope and optimism for a person, a group or for society as a whole, that could be anything from being a comedian to working in a religious organisation fulfilling that sort of role.

Jupiterian careers include: Lawyer, Legislator, Charity worker, Public Service, Welfare services, Wealth and Asset Management, Comedian, Religious, Equine-related occupations, Animal Trainers, Teaching, Education, Travel Agents, Global Business, Flight attendants, Pilots, Interpreters, Publishers, Philosophers, Sea Captains.

Saturn on the Midheaven

Saturn relates to karma and hard work. If you put in the hard work, Saturn gives the reward.

Saturn needs you to develop and demonstrate will power and sometimes also to show restraint. You have to work long and work hard. Saturn can show willpower when we focus the energy of the Sun.

Consider the discipline required for a child to open only one door on a chocolate advent calendar every day—extraordinary willpower for a small child. I also consider the nursery school emphasis on 'sharing' is a big ask: we expect three-year-olds to share toys, but not many parents would be keen to share their car or their jewellery!). Working with Saturn on the MC is not easy.

Saturn is a taskmaster and will require us to become highly practical. You follow Saturn's wisdom and you get rewards. In many ways Saturn is a better 'giver' than Jupiter. Jupiter can 'over promise' or perhaps give us 'too much of a good thing'. Saturn, if you follow his wisdom, is reliable and gives solid rewards. No wishy-washy promises or ideas will do. Saturn wants an input of practical, demonstrable effort and delivers tangible results.

Possible Saturnian careers: Politician, CEO, Business owner, Governmental Roles, Financial Planners, Real Estate Developers, Antique Dealers, Cashiers, Computer Programmers, Archaeological Artefacts.

Uranus on the Midheaven

This is the planet of innovation, of uniqueness, of genius and of flair. Astrology belongs here—Uranus is the modern significator for Astrology. Science and research and anything serving a humanitarian cause belongs to Uranus.

Uranus on the MC will enjoy creating community around their unique specialisms and enjoy their association with that group. They will be unabashed to wear their 'weirdness' with pride and often work independently.

Uranian career fields include: Computers, Innovation, Invention, Programming, 'High Tech', IT, Science, Freelance Business, Activism, Astrology, Engineering and Anything New You Haven't Heard of Yet.

Neptune on the Midheaven

Neptune relates to the dream state, such as fairy stories, Cinderella and Prince Charming. With Neptune here, one has to learn to distinguish the dream state from reality. Being too immersed in fantasy, obsessions develop and people can stray from the avenue to success.

A Neptune MC needs to be on a path of healing, so it is a good placement for medicine and nursing. Neptune rules liquids, so careers to do with water, the oceans, alcohol, and oil all pertain. It is to do with spirituality, art, photography and film, with singing belonging here too.

Possible Neptune on the MC careers are: Television, Celebrity Roles, Singers, Artists, Ceramicists, Actors, Social Workers, Healers, Doctors, Nurses, Prison workers, Facility Managers, Holiday Organisers, Wedding Coordinators, Photographers, Filmmakers, Animators, Marine Professions, Painters, working with the 'underdogs'.

Look to the house that Neptune rules for more indications of the right expression for you.

Pluto on the Midheaven

Pluto is the planet of transformation, the caterpillar to butterfly energy. Pluto has the power of penetration and deep insight. Pluto MC people can penetrate the minds of others and help them transform the negative to positive in some way. With this placement there is an issue of your ability to trust others. You will have to see how this could impact your career success and find ways to mitigate that effect. Pluto is the planet of death, so careers related to death, funeral services etcetera are apt for them. (With a Pluto in Libra on the MC, perhaps you could work doing make-up for corpses, for instance).

Pluto MC people are very intense and can attract powerful people to them (in general they are magnetic and attract things and people). Pluto on the MC may have had extreme experiences of being disempowered in their early life. However, at some point Pluto MC takes their power back and truly owns that power, not just giving an appearance of control.

Pluto is about psychology and digging deep. This placement is good for psychology, hypnotherapy and past life regression. Pluto deals with the invisible, so could relate to finding invisible things or hidden things, researching and uncovering secrets.

Pluto MC careers: Police, Tattoo Artists, Detectives, Sexologists, Politics, Psychology, Funeral Services, Hypnotists, Energy healers, Magicians, Past Life Regression, Taboo Occupations, Espionage, Secret Services.

The Nodes of the Moon are not considered in this book. When the Nodes connect to the MC, it is in fact the *rulership* of the Node that is pertinent.

Aspects to the Midheaven

Sextiles

Planets in sextile to the MC (or AC) can 'turn into money'. They indicate a talent you have to make a conscious choice to develop. With a sextile there is always an issue of choice. It is a Venusian energy. You have to *choose* to use the talent.

Trine

Planets connected to the MC by trine always lead to personal growth. Whether this results in monetary reward depends on other factors, such as the strength of Jupiter in the chart.

Quintiles

Quintiles are 72-degree-aspects. They are another talent aspect, again one that you have to consciously focus on and develop. The problem with quintiles is that sometimes the person doesn't even recognise this talent, it is so natural to them. It won't manifest for you unless you apply yourself and work with it.

Quintile is a Venusian energy (Venus is associated with number five: She goes retrograde in five signs; she takes five positions in solar return charts. She is associated with magic and witchcraft. Consider: apples, seeds, fingers, toes, senses;all five in number).

You have to consider the planets speaking to each other in the quintile aspect:

e.g., Moon quintile Mercury: this could point to singing or writing. (The Moon in traditional astrology ruled writing, in particular writing about emotions and poetry.)

e.g., Moon quintile Pluto talks about success. Moon is talent; Pluto is money, power and success. So, this indicates a talent for achieving success.

e.g., Sun quintile Mars: Sun can represent gold. Mars can relate to digging. So perhaps a gold miner could be indicated here.

e.g., Sun quintile Pluto: This aspect can indicate fame or celebrity.

House and sign positions will be key for coming up with the ideal expression.

e.g., Mars quintile Neptune: Martial arts. (Mars: fighting; Neptune: art/spirituality).

e.g., Jupiter quintile Neptune: Neptune art and spirituality; Jupiter: teaching. So, perhaps a talent for teaching spirituality or art for this combination.

e.g., Saturn quintile Uranus: Saturn the past; Uranus: the future. Possibly astrology because astrology has insight into the past and future.

e.g., Uranus quintile Ascendant: With this aspect the native could be good at identifying and interpreting behaviours. Ascendant: Behaviours. Uranus: deep analysis (as the higher octave of Mercury).

For the quintile talent aspect (72 degrees) you should not use more than a 2-degree orb, very strictly.

Yods

Yods are a special aspect pattern also known as the 'Finger of God' pointing at a planet in your chart that you *must* work with.

The pattern has two quincunxes (inconjuncts) and a sextile, all connected to form a tall, pointy triangle shape.

Quincunx

This is a 150-degree connection; a minor but significant aspect. It was not used in traditional astrology. It is also called an inconjunct. Two planets connected by quincunx have no commonality—not by element, modality or polarity (masculine or feminine orientation). This makes it very difficult to integrate these planetary energies, it will be associated with a degree of discomfort or awkwardness that will require adjustment and adaptation. A quincunx is considered with a maximum orb of 2 or 3 degrees from exactitude.

A quincunx can indicate an area of life where you are either holding back on or overdoing something.

Quincunxes also tend to point to a psychological trauma that developed in childhood when you had no control over the experience.

Planets in Quincunx

The Sun featuring in an inconjunct indicates someone who has no trust in their own intuition and no sense of who they are or who they want to become. Although they want to take on roles, they frequently reject them or, alternatively, find that others reject them. They are always trying to justify themselves, always apologising for simply being.

e.g., With Sun inconjunct Mars, it could be that the father (Sun) challenged or rejected the person.

Moon in an inconjunct suggests the mother is concerned here and was possibly unavailable to the native or emotionally cold. Moon is very private, so this speaks of private or internal matters. It could be related to feelings of shame or embarrassment. There will be a problem of needing approval of others, because the needs sought from the maternal were not forthcoming. The planet quincunxing the Moon will indicate the source of the shame or issue.

e.g., Moon quincunx Mars: a sexual shame; Moon quincunx Venus: shame about loving or sleeping with someone you shouldn't.

Mercury as part of a quincunx shows a problem with communication. There could be a problem with speech; perhaps a speech impediment; perhaps communication blockages in the family; perhaps sibling rivalry problems; needing to be seen as clever, but perceived by others as the opposite; problems with failing at some speaking exercise at school, possibly a recitation or pronunciation that goes wrong. The person suffers from the criticism they have received. Communications are blocked because of these experiences.

With Venus in an inconjunct, it is usually that the self-worth is damaged. Someone did not give the love that was wanted or needed. Possibly there is an experience of being bullied because of appearance. It tends to result in either overgrooming or a complete disregard for the appearance. You want to please others, probably too much. Sign and house placement will give further clues about this quincunx.

Mars in an inconjunct relates to the survival instinct and also to sexuality. You might have been criticised for your sexuality; you could be worried about some sex-related issue, e.g., penis size. There could be problems arising from bad temper. The native might have been subjected to corporal punishment. There might be problems with the immune system. There might have been disappointments where the native has not had the strength to achieve your goals. Mars inconjunct aspects often indicate a holding on to rage that eventually explodes.

Jupiter in an inconjunct indicates issues with boundaries. With this quincunx, it is hard to say no to others, wanting to be helpful. Jupiter wants to grow bigger and bigger and so it overcompensates—does 'anything' for people, because that didn't happen for them: promises were not fulfilled.

They are seeking love from others by doing anything people want.

Saturn in an inconjunct suggests perhaps this person has had too much responsibility thrust upon them at an early age, as a carer or having to look after siblings, and this was felt as a burden. The native might also have felt *they* were a burden to their family. They might have lacked the guidance they needed early on. With this quincunx energy, it can be difficult assuming responsibility as an adult.

A Saturn quincunx can also indicate a predisposition to chronic illnesses. Inconjuncts/Quincunxes in health astrology speak of energies being out of synchronisation, leading to energy blockages and health consequences.

e.g., With a Saturn-Venus inconjunct we experience blockages around relating to others, we don't take responsibility in relationships and feel unworthy of love.

Uranus in an inconjunct suggests moving around a lot and never being able to settle. Natives with a Uranus quincunx can be cast as the 'black sheep of the family'. Often these natives have a hidden shame to deal with. They become unconventional, individualist and rebellious. They can be perceived by others as unreliable, even if they are not. Frequently, they eschew emotional involvement.

Neptune in an inconjunct creates issues with escapism. They can be daydreamers. There could also be drug issues. With a Neptune inconjunction, it is difficult to see situations clearly. The natives can be plagued by self-doubt. Perhaps their parents were unreliable or inconsistent; people *lied* to them. Food drug, alcohol, sex, love, whatever the substance or commodity, can lead to obsession or addiction.

Pluto in an inconjunct denotes a strong hunger for power. Power was denied in childhood. Intense relationships in the family and harsh punishments may have figured. The child will have become afraid of people close to them. It can lead to a fear of change. The connected planet will indicate the sort of change that is frightening to people with this quincunx energy.

Yod

A Yod suggests you are 'chosen by God' for a special purpose, path or challenge.

Start by understanding the planets 'inconjuncting' each other, involved in the Yod pattern. Then add the sextile and whatever talent that suggests. A Yod looks like a witch's hat. A Yod is always a problem and an issue to be addressed. The two planets in sextile indicate something you have to embrace or do, a talent to express. The inconjuncts are the problem(s). The Apex planet (or planets) will show the energy you need to overcome the difficulty. It will be a big challenge.

Planets at the Apex of a Yod

Sun: Chosen to lead

Moon: Chosen to nurture others

Mercury: Chosen to generate ideas, speak, write and use your intellect.

Venus: Chosen to connect people through communicational bridges or to bring two or more objectives together.

Mars: Chosen to pioneer, to take up your sword and fight (symbolically or literally) for a cause.

Jupiter: Chosen to teach others and expand their horizons.

Saturn: Chosen to bear responsibility and help others bear responsibility.

Uranus: Chosen to revolutionise and turn the world upside down in some way.

Neptune: Chosen to inspire others with creativity, mystery and healing. It is a special purpose involving deep mysteries and higher consciousness.

Pluto: Chosen to transform yourself in a phoenix-like way and help others to do this too. You are chosen to resurrect.

Chiron: Chosen to become a healer.

A Yod is a sign of a special mission. It is a mystical symbol of a problem, conundrum or issue in your life and the resolution is related to your purpose in life.

If there is a planet between the two sextile planets this creates a 'Boomerang Yod' and the 'boomerang planet' describes what you must do to solve the problem presented by the Yod.

Remember the main focus in delineating a Yod is the apex planet. This planet indicates the challenge to overcome. Fate will force you to address this issue and when you have overcome this issue, the talent, indicated by the sextile, can manifest.

Stelliums

Stelliums are intense concentrations of planetary influences in one sign or house (3 or 4 planets or more). They are always challenging because this concentration unbalances the chart. Also, the component planets are activated in rapid sequence by any transiting planet and one transits blurs into the next. A person with a stellium on their chart should make a special study of the way to understand and work with stellium energies. I have produced a webinar on Stelliums which will elucidate this special pattern. With a stellium on the MC you probably experience periodic 'firestorms' in your career pathways. Pay particular attention to the lead planet of your stellium.

Coping with stellium experiences takes maturity and strength. Life experience typically leads natives with this configuration to embrace and develop their spirituality—they become 'wise souls'.

Planets Aspecting the Midheaven

Sun Aspecting the Midheaven

The Sun is our lifeforce, our individuality. It can represent a company or 'the boss' in our chart.

Sun is very strong when placed in the 1st or 10th houses. With Sun in the tenth house, the full 'promise' of that Sun placement tends to be activated after 45 or 50 years of age. Sun in the first house is activated earlier, usually by the age of 30.

The house where the Sun is is where you can shine. It is a place you can afford to gamble or take risks; they are more likely to pay off. It is also necessary to check the houses the Sun rules.

The Sun archetypes are the King or Queen, the Owner, the One in Charge, the Chairman of the Board. A very strong Sun suggests a suitability for self-employment, especially if it is aspecting the MC in a cardinal sign.

A strong Sun needs to be a self-starter. It is a proud energy. But it does need to follow through, it can be a great starter and a lousy finisher. There is a tendency to be something of an adrenaline chaser, living life on the edge. A strong Sun in aspect to the MC can benefit from having an assistant, to help with the follow through and temper the tendency to too much risk-taking or over-optimism.

[This differs from a Mars-MC connection. There, the drive is to be challenging and be the best. They are most effective working alone and just sourcing assistance when required. Check if there are Mars as well as Sun aspects.]

Sun-MC needs to embody leadership and help others to shine as much as they shine themselves. Career is very important to them and work energises them. In some capacity they should be working with the public; working at home is unlikely to suit them.

They need to set professional goals and explicitly express what their aims and objectives are. They should use their creativity and connect with others using their particular gifts. They experience learning curves of trial and error as they refine their skills and gifts.

Parental expectation is likely to be a strong influence.

They will attract the spotlight and publicity and ideally stand out for positive rather than negative reasons. Visibility is essential. Garnering applause and developing the right image are priorities.

Creative hobbies may become professions for these natives.

Checking the houses activated by the Sun will give further information; particularly whether those houses are visible to the MC. If the connection is coming from the sixth, for example, the native may experience struggles or even some degree of victimisation. The nature of the aspect to the Sun has to be factored in. An opposition to the MC indicates more of a struggle to integrate and express the solar influence. The Sun does need some time alone to truly connect with who they are; with negative aspects this alone time can become loneliness and isolation.

Sun-MC can be too impulsive or act without enough reflection. Also is it necessary for them to be true authorities in their particular field. With negative aspects they need to be careful not to become too arrogant or self-opinionated, poise and inspiring the liking and trust of others is what brings success. Similarly, being too rebellious will limit success.

A strong Sun is an indicator of a golden touch and an augury of flourishing. It is not, however, a guarantee of success; they have to act. The Sun-MC native should embrace publicity. They have to become the CEO of their own lives. especially if there is a conjunction to the MC or AC.

Possible typically solar careers include: Entertainment, Speculative business, Sport, being a Business Owner or CEO, Cardiologist, Goldsmith, Jeweller, Reality TV, Hair Stylist or Director.

Moon Aspecting the Midheaven

The Moon is a constantly changing body, a shapeshifter. A person with a strong connection of the Moon to the MC or AC is liable to experience ups and downs in their career and they will need to constantly renew themselves. As a reflection of the Moon changing sign by progression every two and half years, these natives will find some changes in their career on the same schedule, new jobs, new roles, new projects will emerge.

The Moon reflects light and has an association with stardom, especially in a Night chart. Conversely it can indicate careers where you work alone.

Writing was considered by the ancients to be associated with the Moon and writing is a lunar career.

Film is associated with the Moon (as well as Neptune). Moon-Neptune aspects are associated with actors and film directors.

For Lunar-MC/AC natives, following the movements of the progressed Moon is vital.

Moon rules the public, in a manner described by the sign. The Moon describes the public image of a company and a Moon in aspect to the MC or AC creates someone who is customer-focused (it rules demographic studies, for instance), a people-pleaser, especially with Capricorn or Libra. With a connection to Mercury or Jupiter we could be a good intuitive marketer.

A strong Moon should be tuned into the financials of a company, especially in Taurus or Scorpio or in the second or eighth, sixth, or twelfth.

The Moon is a container: relates to alcohol (bottle); real estate (house). It speaks of the creation of tribes.

A connection to Ceres might suggest starvation, food industry or food business, or charity feeding programmes.

Work involving the intuition is suggested by an angular Moon.

Writing is suggested especially when there is an influence of Mercury and Jupiter. Music is a lunar occupation, especially when Neptune is implicated.

Meanings of the Moon:

Feeling-Home-Family-Food-Mood-Emotions-Health-Fertility-Energy/Motivation-Unseen or hidden things-Opportunity-Intuition-Writing-Monday-Potato, lettuce, cabbage, cucumber, cauliflower,-Taste of cucumber and water-Smell of water and the forest-Containers-Finances-Women and sensitive people-Music-Writing-Emotional decisions-Blue Monday-Women's cycles-Gardening-the Human Body-Luna-lunacy-lunatics.

If the Moon is near an angle, the person will play a 'connector' role or may play a maternal role for others in some way. They can be leaders, but they will be empathic leaders who lead by their emotional connections to people.

An angular Moon may predispose people to being manipulative, but potentially in a positive way: keeping people happy for promoting good outcomes and making 'people-first' decisions.

The Moon is also concerned with security and sometimes climbing ladders creates emotional security. A stressed or poorly aspected Moon can lash out when stressed or become overly emotionally invested in the outcomes of projects. Like an angular Mars, they can fail to finish things. They are at the mercy of moods.

As managers they bring a team together and refine and nurture the emotional core connection by being giving and caring. They are successful at this when they are able to show their own vulnerabilities. They may change their (public) name.

The Sun is the secret of sanity and the Moon is the secret of happiness.

Mercury Aspecting the Midheaven

Mercury deals with ideas, sales and the conveying and processing of information. It has no gender and it has no loyalty. It is associated with rapid changes and is depicted with winged feet.

Mercury is of course the trickster energy, a playful energy. It is related to writing, speaking, printing, wit and humour. In a company setting, Mercury would emphasise marketing, especially with a connection with Pluto, Jupiter or the second house. It would rule marketing, telecoms and sales, phone communications, and transportation.

Mercury needs variety and thrives juggling multiple tasks. It is all about communication. Facilitation, training and teaching are Mercurial occupations. They are adept with formulas and methods. Writing. Especially short length writing is associated with Mercury, including things like newsletters.

A strong angular Mercury can make money using verbal, intellectual and artistic skills. Schools and agencies are suitable locations. They can deal easily with contracts, statements, spreadsheets, costings and balances and work well on a commission basis or in a bonus system.

The flexibility of Mercury is one of their key assets.

They are the bridge builders, especially in one to one connections. A Mercury-MC person excels at deals and negotiations.

They need to scrupulously avoid being drawn into gossip; it will harm them. A negatively-aspected Mercury doubts their knowledge or can ignore the opinions of others or even tell lies. Misusing their communication skill will certainly lead to failure. Their communication needs to be fact-based and they need to share opinions with others. They need mental stimulation and humour. Often with a Mercury-MC connection, the mother is very smart and the native somehow wants to honour their mother's intelligence.

Venus Aspecting the Midheaven

A Venus MC aspect often is a social butterfly. They are bridge builders too, but where Mercury unites individuals, Venus brings together groups. They need to use their beauty, creativity, feminine qualities (whether male or female) and employ their charm and seductive nature. This could be with their body or their voice.

They thrive surrounded by luxury and things and environments that are beautiful, harmonious, expensive and tasteful. They need to personally appear as smart and well put-together and demonstrate their inner sexiness.

In connection to Jupiter or Neptune, Venus on the angles needs to watch the finances. They are prone to extravagance and losses.

Venus is related to sweets, luxury goods, textiles, fashion and furnishings. In connection to Pallas Athena or Jupiter it can suggest legal careers. It is also related to artistic endeavours and occupations that are very social or related to entertainment.

Venus in the second house is all about money, but with the attendant danger of over-indulgence.

The career for the Venus-MC person has to be associated with the personal value system, otherwise they come to find their work robotic.

They insist on a working environment of mutual respect, with good manners and kindness being demonstrated. They have to refine, integrate and use their own social skills.

Venus on the MC can become famous via their partners or through their personal beauty.

With negative aspects from Venus to the MC, there could be problems if the person is manipulative, plays people against each other or constantly demands validation from others. They can 'kiss asses' and be lazy and overly people-pleasing. Often when young they struggled to be taken seriously.

It can be that these people are raised in family environments where they have to act as mediators, between parents or other family members.

Mars Aspecting the Midheaven

Mars is always important in a career, even when it is not strong. This is because it describes your motivations.

A Gemini Mars is searching for information, a Cancer Mars wants to be, and to experience, caring. Jupiter and Mars in trine suggests good instincts for buying. Saturn and Mars in bad aspect suggest poor buying skills.

Mars is an individualist, assertive or even aggressive. They see themselves as leaders, but can be reluctant to wait and climb the ladder to leadership positions. In this way Mars meets opposition. If too aggressive they, of course, fail.

A strong Mars is great for competition and ambition, for sport and in combat. They need to use their magnetism and sometimes take physical action.

Mars in relation to Neptune or Venus could suggest a drummer. Mars is associated with scars, wounds, guns, knives, and other weapons. They can be soldiers and fighters, but they need to be strategists too. Mars in aspect to the Moon or Ceres, might, for example, influence working with eating disorders. Mars means "fighting" and "Ceres" means food. This can help us navigate and potentially overcome our fight with food.

Mars is often a double-edged sword.

An angular Mars person has often been obliged to leave the family early and strike out on their own. Or their mothers could have encouraged them to be assertive.

The position of Mars in the chart shows where you need to be brave and get up quickly when you fail. This is the area of life where you need to show up. Stand up, struggle and fight a good fight. Wherever Mars is, it calls for bravery.

Mars careers can include physical labour, skills training, or being a warrior: anywhere you need to combine strategy and effort. They are also good with cars and property.

Mars has to learn patience and the discretion to live to fight another day. They can be 'know-it-all' when young. They want to be leaders and call the shots. They resist categorisation and can demonstrate artistic abilities.

They should capitalise on a strong sexual identity. They are best working independently and hate to be micromanaged.

A badly-aspected Mars can be brutal or violent (perhaps having witnessed this at home). They might also tend to be arrogant.

Jupiter Aspecting the Midheaven

It might be assumed Jupiter in aspect to the MC is necessarily positive, but it has its drawbacks too. Mythologically, Jupiter is the only surviving son of Saturn. It is also associated with the Norse god Thor, the thunderbolt.

Where Jupiter is in a chart is where you get the most return from your effort. It is where you have an archangel backing you up. Jupiter has a 'grand vision'.

Jupiter relates to careers to do with the foreign, with operating on a world platform such as in an international business. It is associated with marketing, global trade and publishing. It wants to travel and connect with foreign cultures.

Jupiter can be a bit greedy and with a strong Jupiter in aspect to the MC the native must take care not to cut corners, it will backfire.

A transit of Jupiter will indicate where to invest time, effort or money. A poor Jupiter fears not being able to expend, to create, grow and is fearful of wasting money.

Suitable fields for the Jupiterian MC are: professional fields, business, mass media, advertising, teaching, large companies, law, religion, and philosophy. A strong Jupiter demonstrates its 'royal' nature, and affords financial protection. Jupiter can relate to writing too (as well as Moon and Mercury). It indicates abundance, especially in connection to Pluto, the second house and earth signs.

Jupiter MC has a talent for management and leadership. They need someone who believes in them, mentors and role models. They have to 'give back' too, if they don't, they invite failure. They can be star-makers, spotting talent and helping others to help themselves. They need to exhibit positivity at all times and share their wealth and success, as well as make things happen for others, in a way, playing the role of the gods.

They want people to believe in them and they want to return the favour.

Jupiter influenced by Pluto or Neptune can become famous because of a scandal and this can promote or detract from their success.

Jupiter can also be over-optimistic or hang on to projects with no future. They might also tend to over-promising. Jupiter shows its greedy side when something is missing, something of real meaning. It could be fifth house things: a child, adventure, romance.

A Jupiter MC can often have come from a wealthy or successful family. Education will be important to them, but they may or may not finish a degree. Jupiter can be larger than life and sometimes the mother was an overwhelming figure.

Saturn Aspecting the Midheaven

Saturn in mythology was the father of Jupiter and child of Gaia the Earth Mother, Uranus (his father) did not stay around to help. Saturn was sent by Gaia to kill his father Uranus. Saturn does have a jealous side, but also a moral compass; he wants to be able to justify his actions and create order out of chaos.

With Saturn aspecting the MC we need to become a master of our profession. We strive to leave a legacy. There is a gift for business and business structure and building something. It is possible to excel in fields such as real estate and work involving stone or ice. It makes for a capable manager. Another suitable work is any related to older people. Saturn-MC is prepared to work hard with patience and perseverance. Time and money and effort will yield success and Saturn is ready to put that in.

With Saturn in a chart angle, the native is likely to be a late bloomer. Capricorn, the sign Saturn rules, is a Sea-Goat, a double-bodied creature, half fish and half mountain goat. Thus, it covers the world from the depths of the ocean to the top of the mountains. As a double-bodied sign, this reflects the two proclivities in Capricorn: In the first 15° of Capricorn, there is a desire to work with people. In the last 15° the native is more hermit-like and more suited to working alone.

Saturn is rarely recognised as a talent planet, but it is. Saturn will ask: Are you building fortitude or building on your fears? It has a bad reputation. As the 'greater malefic' it is seen as bringing restriction, and raising barriers. It does need boundaries, but these don't have to be obstacles. Saturn can indicate a fear of failure, lack of confidence and long delays. The native with the Saturn aspect to the MC must face frustration and be ready to bear the burden. There may be wrong thinking about not deserving money, unreasonable fears of loss, or with poor aspects from the 12th or 2nd house, beliefs that money is corrupting.

Those with this signature can succeed in trade and management and want to build security. The educational options you choose tend to involve long study. The native needs to be able to analyse risk (especially with a Scorpio connection) and be ready to take the necessary risks to achieve success.

Financial discipline is key. The Saturn MC can never cheat—the karma is swift. They will have to conquer their terrors. Saturn rules companies; the Saturnian company is one that survives when others crumble.

The idea for the Saturn aspected MC is to become the CEO of their own life. They need a clear mission and goals that are written down and ticked off as they are achieved. There is a desire to do something that makes the world a better place.

They will resist labels and crystallise their own identity. They will have to tackle issues of self-confidence and learn not to take into account what others think. They are challenged to interact with the world and take the heat.

The Saturn-MC person is wise beyond their years and plays by the rules. Others fooling around at work annoys them. They are hard workers from a very early age. If they somehow think they don't deserve success and happiness, they refuse help and keep people at a distance. They succeed by connecting positively with authority figures. They behave obediently and act as the timekeepers for others.

The family often casts a shadow for these individuals. They are determined not to be like their father.

Uranus Aspecting the Midheaven

In the myths, Uranus was the sky God and the consort of Gaia. He is central to creation stories. Uranus is associated with big modern organisations, with the download of universal information, with Big Ideas and 'ah-ha!' moments. He rules lightning bolts, electric shocks to the consciousness, magic and alchemy. He relates to large groups and social networks. Uranus is emotionally detached, not because there is no emotion felt, but because of a fear of rejection. Aquarius, the sign ruled by Uranus in modern astrology, is the Water Bearer. He wants to connect, but is afraid.

Uranus-MC people do not fit in until they accept, embrace and celebrate their uniqueness. They don't need to fit in, they just need to find a job where they can express their uniqueness.

Uranus on the angles, or highly aspected, experiences a significant change every seven years. Uranus relates to a seven year business cycle.

The qualities of Uranus are: eccentricity, extremism, unorthodoxy and in general being an outsider. They need to find a golden middle road which tempers their more extreme energies.

Suitable fields are science, art, counselling, human resources, high technology, working at civil or government contracts. Uranus has unique talents and originality. They are likely to experience gains and losses, especially if there is a 2nd house connection. The same 2nd house connection can bring overnight success.

They will feel the need to engage with a humanitarian cause. They are likely to excel in an unusual job that gives them freedom. They are well suited to being entrepreneurs. They need a mentally stimulating environment where it is okay to be unconventional. They have genius, out-of-the-box ideas and achieve things that benefit society.

Uranus is also associated with shame. They don't need to be ashamed of their career or their uniqueness.

Chiron Aspecting the Midheaven

Many consider Chiron, the centaur, to be the ruler of Virgo.

A prominent Chiron on the angles can point to a tragic life, or at least having a tragic event impact their lives and, of course, therefore their career. Chiron on the MC often works too hard and damages their health. They give too much. Often everyone can identify the issues, except the native themselves. There can be a lot of drama in work life.

Working in health care and with the healing arts can be great for them. These people often attract wounded people in their personal lives who can bring them down, because they give way too much. They can put all their eggs in one basket and that fails them.

The best advice when they are suffering is not to get lost in licking their own wounds, but instead to go out and heal others.

Suitable work includes healing karmic and family wounds (especially if there is Pluto, Neptune or Moon connections). They can be excellent corporate consultants.

There is a sort of Mars and Jupiter quality to Chiron, too.

Chiron MC people tend to be very intelligent and are good at giving advice. They make excellent holistic practitioners, drug and alcohol counsellors and weight management consultants.

Chiron is famously the 'rainbow bridge' between Saturn and Uranus, giving a particular view of current and future reality and keen foresight.

Neptune Aspecting the Midheaven

Neptune, also called Poseidon, is the God of the Sea. Like the sea, Neptune is endless and without boundaries. Neptune believes in the impossible.

In an earth sign, Neptune on the angles can be very stubborn, quite lost and acts to defeat itself.

In the business world Neptune rules mergers and large scale re-organisations. It can also represent a heavy debt and a business that is part of a much larger group of companies.

Suitable Neptunian careers could include: nautical products or jobs, dealing with oil, petrol, paint, rubber or gas; also wine, drugs, or other pharmaceuticals. Neptune MC natives could do well as holistic or traditional healers and work in hospitals, hospices, orphanages, asylums, prisons or with the homeless. They work well with addictions, obsessions and in careers related to the feet.

As Neptune is the planet of illusions, Neptune-MC is a great placement for photographers, dancers, musicians or make-up artists. They might excel in the field of dream analysis or hypnotherapy.

They can have their head in the clouds and do not want to be burdened with too much responsibility, so it is a placement for a good delegator!

They like to use their kindness and compassion, even a degree of seductiveness, but must be careful not to fall into unhealthy roles as saviours, martyrs or making too many sacrifices. They yearn to escape domesticity and perhaps to achieve fame and become celebrated.

It is a good aspect for actors, singers, filmmakers and artists.

There is in some sense a need to forgive and to give to society. With Neptune on an angle, though, people don't see who you actually are, they see an illusion, which is often an attractive illusion. People with a Neptune-MC aspect have to avoid self-defeating attitudes or behaviours. It is important to limit themselves to just one or two projects. With difficult aspects the Neptune MC can tell lies or misrepresent themselves, as well as being susceptible to deception.

Neptune is behind the American Dream. Work options that could work are being an influencer, working in the media, and especially fighting for the underdog, if not being the underdog themselves. They may take unwise risks and lose money. They want to be seen as beautiful souls.

Unfortunately, Saturn the bubble-popper comes round regularly and then the Neptune MC can feel stupid or naïve.

Often the native had very idealising parents or a mother who sacrificed for the family, perhaps giving up their career. Or the mother might have abandoned the family.

Pluto Aspecting the Midheaven

Pluto aspecting the MC gives a native who needs to reclaim their power. Somehow their power was stolen and they go on to get it back in the shape of wealth, success and recognition. It is an aspect associated with huge ups and downs and some major fears.

A person with this placement needs to examine and assess their personal power and resources and find ways to unlock their potential. They do this by continual rebirth and re-inventing themselves, especially if Pluto conjuncts the MC.

There may be skeletons in the closet acting as career blocks.

Pluto is a planet of darkness and also light. Pluto is associated with Lucifer, the Fallen Angel. By finding their personal strength, they see the human dimension, not just monsters under the bed.

Pluto in aspect to the MC gives a laser-focus on the career. They may excel in the corporate world, be high achievers and be the object of intense family or societal pressure, politics is a Plutonian field where they can find themselves the object of public hatred. In some way they could change how people understand death.

Pluto MC people may have been expected to excel, perhaps having parents who pushed them to succeed. They will certainly benefit from psychological insights.

They attract or are themselves power-hungry people. They are born to be the alchemists and agents of change in the world. Outer success can come at the cost of sacrifice of inner desires. They should use their strong sexual charisma. Careers focused on mysteries and investigations are a place they can thrive.

Outer planets within 3° of the angles are very impactful, being experienced then in the personal sphere, not just as collective energies. The North and South Nodes are also career indicators; with the nodes we mainly consider the conjunction to the MC.

The North Node has a Jupiterian flavour, the South Node a Saturnian or Chironic character.

Solar Aspects
and the Life Mission

The Sun is of incalculable importance in the natal chart and is strangely overlooked by many astrologers, beyond the basic meaning of the Sun's sign placement.

The Sun describes vitality, vocation and the father figure, but also your mission: what you have 'signed up for' in this lifetime. The Sun describes your calling, your identity and what you should be striving for and moving toward in life. The Sun talks about what makes your heart sing.

The Sun's aspects point to what we have to do to accomplish our mission.

Sometimes, early in life, we express the opposite polarity to our Sun sign. An Aquarius Sun, for example, will want ultimately to become a reformer and to develop great independence, but it will learn through the Leo energies.

Sun is often mistaken for indicating the obvious characteristics, when in fact the Rising sign and the Moon sign are most often your visible qualities. You live the Rising and Moon sign energies, especially at the beginning of your life.

After 33, when the Sun matures it begins to show itself, the Sun traits show themselves.

The importance of the Sun often gets overlooked. Aspects of the Sun give the best indication of 'why you were born'. They are indications of your purpose in life.

Trines and sextile aspects indicate things that help you fulfil your destiny. Squares and oppositions suggest the problems in your path, especially the ones you encounter early in life.

Sun-Pluto Aspects

Sun and Pluto aspects often indicate an introverted individual. These people have extraordinary willpower and are very structured in approach to things. They are aware of what they want, having deep insight. It can be hard to contain or harness Sun-Pluto energy. It could indicate psychic abilities. These natives feel the collective energies and that can be difficult or overwhelming.

If the power of the Sun-Pluto energy is not integrated within, it can be met from the outside as aggression etc.

It is an aspect of great potential, for personal growth and for regrowth. Whatever is thrown at Sun-Pluto, they can get up and begin again. They learn to admit failures and mistakes, after which they cannot affect them anymore. Sun-Pluto people dealt with difficult or abusive situations at the hands of others early in life leaving them with feelings of shame and embarrassment. They may have feared for their very survival. They have to overcome these feelings and get their power back. These people will dig deep to understand what happened to them and learn how to stop people manipulating them. Through this experience, Sun-Pluto not only takes back their own power, but they learn to empower others. They know how to turn negatives into positives. They may have once been bullied or subjected to humiliations, but can become the people who uncover the oppression of others.

Sun symbolises the light, Pluto, the darkness. The Sun is heaven, Pluto, the underworld. Sun-Pluto embodies the Great Transformer who can reconcile these huge polarities. With an opposition Sun-Pluto aspect, the native processes and reconciles these experiences externally in interactions with others. With a square aspect, the native completes the process more internally.

Pluto also represents hostage situations, being held against your will; the Sun-Pluto individual may feel this way about their personal history.

Sun-Pluto has trust issues. Their trust is betrayed in formative years and in consequence, they don't trust themselves. Until this is resolved, this is projected in relationships. They don't trust their partners. Sun-Pluto energy is intensely magnetic and if they have a core belief that precludes trust, they can draw to themselves experiences that mirror that insecurity within, attracting partners who cheat and betray them. Pluto can represent infidelity. Sun represents the father archetype and Sun-Pluto has father complexes, so possibly may feel the Father betrayed them.

Pluto always survives. They may 'take the bullet' for others in these experiences. They might even be able to forgive, but Pluto will never, never forget what happened.

Pluto is also the planet of obsession. In addition to an obsession of any sort they have to ask themselves what they are trying to compensate for.

Nearly always the obsession relates to childhood trauma.

Sun-Uranus Aspects

Uranus relates to astrology, but before these natives find Astrology, they experience a lot of changes and sudden, traumatic and unexpected situations. Sun-Uranus pushes from within too, to make the native change things. The energy at play is hectic and dynamic. When Uranus aspects the Sun it can destabilise your life mission and long-term goals. There is a requirement for intense focus.

On the plus side, the Uranian influence can give lucid thinking, sharp objectivity and clear long-term goals. It sees a way forward. Ultimately, Sun-Uranus *will* come to a stage of progress.

With the Sun in a hard aspect to Uranus, squares and oppositions, we see natives who are 'ahead of their time'. They are full of brilliant innovative ideas. However, they find it hard to sell these ideas to others and Sun-Uranus meets with rejection. As young people, these natives may feel they are born in the wrong time and place. They frequently clash with authority figures. They feel misunderstood and unheard.

Sun-Uranus must learn to respect their inner truth and their individuality. They are individuality personified; unique and quirky. They are often very rebellious, especially when young. Once they harness these energies and trust themselves within, they begin to understand that most people are simply not ready for their ideas. They will always be 'outsiders' to some extent. Others might experience them as rather intense to be around.

They are the reformers and catalysts who are here to improve the world. They see the world from another angle and create new and alternative paths for others. They are here to shake things up. (Uranus rules earthquakes, volcanoes and similar phenomena.) They are here to wake us up. They think outside the box and many are hugely intelligent or even geniuses, but perhaps this is not recognised or understood. They are not bound by conventions or traditions: they are ground-breakers and pioneers. They create change.

Most often they are better not working for others, but finding a way to operate more independently.

If the Sun-Uranus person finds themselves at a crossroads, with a big life decision to make, they must ask very seriously what is the right decision for *them*. After chaotic early life experiences where they may have moved a lot (especially if there are Moon contacts too), in the later part of life Sun-Uranus people get themselves stuck trying to avoid re-experiencing the turmoil of their childhood. However, they need to cut away any block to their individuality or they are blocking their 'mission' too.

With the humanitarian focus of Uranus, Sun-Uranus natives can be highly philanthropic. Any activity out of the norm is liable to suit. They need to embrace spontaneity and live on the edge. Stability and routines are never going to work for them.

Sun-Uranus can also become the black sheep of their families. But they are here to break family patterns and cycles. They put the truth on the table. In childhood they maybe did not fit in, but they have to overcome fears of not fitting in. They have to even go against the whole community, at times, because they have to be true to themselves.

Sun-Uranus is the first person to jump up and dance at a party. Eventually we are all up on the floor.

Sun-Neptune Aspects

Sun-Neptune people are our visionaries. They are artistic and dreamy and *very* emotional. In fact, they have to be emotionally connected to what they do or they will not be able to sustain it.

Neptunian energy is amorphous and elusive and vague. Neptune does not always want to be in the public eye, it wants to hide away. Sun, however, wants to shine. The Sun is logical, Neptune is lost in emotion. In fact, Neptune can tune into the emotions of the collective and that can be overwhelming.

Sun-Neptune people are frequently overwhelmed, prey to all sorts of fears (their own and those of others). They fall into victim-saviour role traps.

They need to appreciate how their ability to connect emotionally with others is their 'superpower'. They see how the world is interconnected. They have an instinctive grasp of the 'oneness' of things.

They will probably be happiest devoting themselves to healing and helping others, but must respect their need to withdraw and recharge their batteries periodically. The Sun shines, Neptune withdraws.

Neptune is the higher octave of Venus, the planet of love. Venus is earthly love; Neptune is divine love. Sun-Neptune people are here to connect others to the power of divine love. Any type of spiritual work or practice works for them.

These natives have a chameleon quality, the ability to tune in and slip into the thoughts, feelings, moods and behaviours of others. They adapt to situations. This is a great pairing for actors and actresses.

The downfall of Sun-Neptune is the problem of maintaining boundaries. They don't know how to say 'No'. Neptune rules obsession. Substances, drugs, and alcohol can pose problems. Sun-Neptune people are highly susceptible to influences etc. Neptune is about escapism, even escaping their own true path. Sometimes the Sun-Neptune person overcompensates and erects overly rigid boundaries. The key is balance: strong boundaries that still allow emotion and inspiration to flow in and out.

The Dalai Lama has Sun and Neptune in sextile, so these energies are more easily reconciled for him. For people with the square and opposition it is harder to see how they are here to help others.

Remember that early in life we tend to live the polarity of our Sun. Supposing you had the Sun in Pisces: In early life you might exhibit Virgo traits. Later in life, you can set aside your analysing and quantifying tendencies; when you are living your spirituality, you don't need to systematise in a Virgo way.

It is also important for Sun-Neptune people to realise they don't have to (in fact can't) save everyone. They are here to guide people and point out the right road forwards. They have to take responsibility because Sun wants to take responsibility; however, Neptune blurs the boundaries and takes on responsibility when it should not.

Sun-Neptune people have fabulous imaginations. This signature is great for design, writing, art and music. With Venus contact too they might be gifted singers. These creative expressions will be the antidote to addictive tendencies.

Sun-Neptune (conjunction especially) feels they are too emotional for others to bear, but in fact they are the ones struggling with the emotions, not others.

Neptune is the planet of muses. Inspiration is their lifeblood. When inspired they have no need for addictions or obsession. They need to know inspiration comes and goes and not panic or resort to substances or unhelpful behaviours trying to recapture inspiration. Often, they just need to rest, then the muse returns.

The opposite polarity to Pisces is Virgo. Sun-Neptune people need to take care of their body (a Virgoan concern) so they are able to effectively channel all the spiritual energies.

Neptune loves singing, dancing, music and film, all these things delight and calm them and could be part of their life path.

Sun-Saturn Aspects

Sun-Saturn people are born wise old souls. Saturn does have boundaries. It is wise and mature. Saturn talks about discipline and focus. Unfortunately, Saturn does not allow the Sun to have fun and Sun (Leo) does need fun.

Perhaps these natives took on responsibility very early and were restricted and could not play. Perhaps they did not have a strong Father figure or, conversely, had a very authoritarian Father. Either way this can unbalance them and lead to self-doubt. Properly integrated, Sun-Saturn energy gives great discipline, focus and perseverance. It allows for a steady, methodical progress towards long-term goals. Saturn ultimately does help to achieve goals. In the end they can be authority figures for others and serve as an example to others. They need to learn to take care of themselves in the process.

Saturn close to the Sun can have issues with seeing things clearly, especially at the early part of life. There are limits on what you see, under the blinding rays of the Sun. Another analogy is wine—the older the wine, the better the taste. This pairing is linked to ageing and wisdom.

After the age of forty, these people have their best years. Early they may have had father issues (Saturn represents father in a night chart and Sun represents father in a day chart) or suffered harsh experiences (especially with hard aspects). Saturnian efforts and hard work, leaves them well placed to achieve goals. Sun-Saturn is the classic leadership signature.

Sun-Jupiter Aspects

Jupiter speaks to us of exoticism, natural justice and faith. Sun and Jupiter energies have things in common and can blend very well. There is a tendency to be over-optimistic or running after 'false prophets'. They need to make a reality check to be sure of the value of what they are chasing.

Jupiter and the Sun both have a lot of energy. Sun-Jupiter people need to watch self-indulgence in order to protect their bodies. Another possible downfall is being over-generous or spending unwisely. But they can be great motivators and leaders. They can inspire others when they have true belief in what they teach. It is the signature of a guru figure, even.

They can understand philosophies and how to share them with others. The Sun is about logic and clarity; Jupiter is about higher learning. Sharing higher wisdom might be their life mission.

Sun and Jupiter are both royal energies. They can also indicate fame. Certainly they 'live life large and loud'. There is an exuberance about this energy.

With a tendency to greed and being spendthrift, it is best if these natives learn about money management early in life to avoid difficulties. Jupiter magnifies good or bad traits.

As young people Sun-Jupiter may be seeking meaning in life, travelling and moving and changing jobs often. They become gipsies or adventurers. They need a firm belief inside about what they have signed up to do in this life.

Sun-Jupiter has a very generous and benevolent spirit. They can be good lawyers and solicitors and university teachers, sharing their knowledge for the good of others. They want to encourage and help others. They need new experiences and variety. They are fascinated by other cultures and philosophies. They could be good at writing books or need to share their knowledge in some way. Sun-Jupiter is associated with Big Ideas. One pitfall is that they can set the bar too high in life and if they fail it can be hard to pick themselves up.

Sun-Mars Aspects

Natives with the hard aspects between Sun and Mars may have experienced aggression early in life.

These people are the initiators. They have high energy, also *lots* of physical energy and need lots of movement and being out and about. They are pioneers. Sun-Mars is into competition, big time. They have to find a way to be in the driving seat of their life. They are supposed to take the lead. It is a 'DIY' planetary combination. Sun-Mars people need to learn early that you can fall down without being defeated: You can get up and keep fighting.

They need to stick up for someone, themselves, others or a cause of some kind. They want to fight for what is important.

Early in life Sun-Mars might have had to fight for survival or identity. They might have been seen as underdogs, but they have a competitive spirit and want to achieve. They need to find outlets for their anger and their physical energy or this can lead to illness. They are risk takers, so they have to be reasonable about risk. They need to do what is *worth* doing, not doing for doing's sake. Mars cannot be combusted by the Sun. It can take the heat.

Both are hot and dry fire energies.

Mars represents logic and conjunct the Sun the logic can be blurred. With the conjunction, Mars does not lose *strength* but it does lose *vision*.

There is a high level of energy available for achievement, but Sun-Mars needs to find the right thing to achieve.

Rescue work would be good work for them. Lifeguards, police and firemen fight to protect others, so these roles satisfy that need to fight. Sun-Mars might be striving for the underdog in life or they might be fighting for the underdog.

Sun-Venus Aspects

Venus is the ruler of both Taurus and Libra. With a Sun and Venus connection there can be Taurean or Libran expressions of the Venusian energy and sometimes both. There is an emphasis on looking good; on how things 'look' in general. The Sun's desire to shine, its willpower and self-image focus is united with the Venusian need for harmony and artistic presentation. Even a Sun-Venus that looks like a toad will be a very good-looking toad.

The worlds of fashion and art can attract these natives. There can be an interest in food (a Taurean enthusiasm) and often have a marked sweet tooth and a tendency to indulgence.

With the conjunction there is typically a decided vanity. Squares and Oppositions might have issues around self-worth.

Sun-Venus needs to 'find the love' inside themselves, not constantly seek outside validation. They need to appreciate their own strength and value. With the Sun's need to shine and the Venusian need for everything to go smoothly, these natives compromise too much and are diplomatic to a fault. They can reduce themselves to 'people pleasers' who have forgotten their own goals and only serve others. They learn to say 'no' to people, when something is not in their interest.

Libran ruled Venus gives Sun-Venus a talent for bringing people together. They are bridge builders making connections between people with similar interests. They do this by making relationships, differently from the way Mercury networks, which is all about the information shared.

Sun-Venus succeeds when they build relationships of peace and harmony in which the self-worth and gifts of all parties are honoured.

They excel at any sort of one-to-one consultation activity including legal work of course, with the Libran imperative for justice and fairness.

Venus never travels far from the Sun, not beyond 47 degrees. Thus, the only possible aspects for Sun-Venus are the conjunction and the semi-square. So even when Sun-Venus is the closest aspect, it is good in this case to also explore the next closest aspect, to give the clearest picture of the route to success.

Sun-Mercury Aspects

Mercury the messenger thrives in careers to do with communications, the internet and anything using writing skills.

Mercury is another planet who never strays far from the Sun. The only possible aspect is the conjunction and we only consider it a conjunction with a tight orb.

Mercury close to the Sun leaves the mercurial talents obscured, hidden or bleached out by the solar light. This can leave the native difficulties with expression of their thoughts and ideas. These natives might have been slow to develop their communication skills compared to others. They might have felt unheard or not understood as children. They could have had challenges like speech impediments. Sometimes there was poor communication in the family. Perhaps there were lots of taboo subjects and no one spoke about anything important. This will affect their clarity of mind.

Early experiences lead Sun-Mercury people to doubt themselves. Sometimes they compensate for this doubt by becoming opinionated, insisting that people accept what they say, when in fact they need to listen to others, because, really, they want to learn. Knowledge is very important to them. They have the capacity to become great researchers.

Like Sun Venus, Sun-Mercury are great at bringing people together. They share ideas and phone numbers and links and they introduce people to each other.

Sun-Moon Aspects

Sun Moon aspects are a topic beyond the scope of this book, they need a book of their own to do them justice, so are not considered here.

Unaspected Sun

In this case the qualities of the Sun sign shine very purely. It is similar to having a Sun at zero degrees of a sign. They both present the sign in its essence.

It is not an easy thing, because the Sun receives no support. However, if the native comes to accept their inner truth, they will shine, like the Sun. An Unaspected Sun suggests the native has a big mission that might be hard to fulfil. It is quite rare to have an unaspected Sun.

It can indicate a missing father and the absence of any father figure in the native's life, which is challenging. There are no role models to emulate or challenge. On the positive side, the native is free to create their own destiny.

I have an unaspected Sun. In early years I lived out my 'solar-polar' Leo qualities, working hard in a gregarious outgoing environment, assuming leadership roles. I was not ready for the mission of the unaspected Sun in Aquarius on the 12th. With maturity I learned the power of solitude. I discovered I did not need to be a leader of others and became instead a leader in my own life, assuming Aquarian independence and succeeding well in self-employment in the very Aquarian sphere of Astrology. Finally finding the right expression for my talents and energies is fantastically rewarding.

Even the most challenging Sun aspects are helpers. They help you to come home to yourself.

The house position of the Sun shows *where* you would most like to shine and should put in efforts to develop or express your Sun energy. To see the results of our efforts, see the house where there is Leo on the cusp i.e., the house the Sun rules. Here we see the expression of the Sun and see how we are achieving.

Lunar Nodes in the Houses and Vocation

The Lunar North Node is an important point in the chart. It is highly significant to the 'life mission' and vocation.

For the vocational astrologer, when it seems the client is not responding or recognising Midheaven indicators, and resisting the MC promise of ease and success, look to the North Node.

The North Node is a point in space where the orbit of the Moon intersects with the Ecliptic (Path of the Earth around the Sun). Thus, it is a fusion of Solar and Lunar influences.

It relates to invisible and unseen forces, cosmic forces, that affect the native and is related closely to their 'Karmic Contract', what their soul signed up to achieve in this lifetime.

In a 28-day Moon cycle, the Moon spends half of the cycle in the northern celestial hemisphere and half in the southern. Where it passes from one hemisphere to the other are the North (ascending) and South (descending) Nodes.

The astrologer has the choice of working with the True or Mean Node. The True Node is the actual position of the node. The Mean Node 'evens out' the highly erratic path of the nodes to show general progression. I prefer to work with the True Node.

Esoterically there are four major categories of Karma:

Sanchita Karma which is the total accumulated karma of all past lives, *PrarabdhaKarma* which is karma which will affect us in this lifetime, *Kriyamana Karma* which is the karma we create in this lifetime and *Agama Karma* which is the Karma we create for future lives.

The first two types relate to the Lunar South Node.

The second two types of karma relate to the Lunar North Node.

The North Node spends approximately 18 months in a sign (the South Node is always at the exact opposite pole of the chart from the

North Node). This polar axis is called the Axis of Fate. It describes our karma and our destiny.

Following the direction of our North Node will move us in the direction of success and happiness in life. Like the Moon, the North Node is an indicator of what we need to do to be happy. It is essential to follow the North Node and Lunar directions.

The North Node has a Jupiterian quality. Think mountain top or elevated position. It is also known as the 'Dragon's Head' or in Vedic astrology as 'Rahu'. It is the entry point for cosmic energies that bring progress. It is a 'cup that overflows' but much depends on our ability to respond and take in these energies. It is also a point where we are greedy and hungry for experiences, but the energies are challenging to integrate.

The South Node conversely has a Saturnine quality. It is very hard to leave the expressions of the South Node point behind. It can indicate talents and proclivities we bring from previous lives, but we need to move towards the North Node polarity in life and not get stuck in the comfort zone of the South Node. This is the Dragon's Tail point where there are things to be released and left behind. Success depends on our ability to liberate ourselves from that past life karma and grow. It describes an area where we may feel a burdensome responsibility or restriction, sometimes where we have the need to make sacrifices. The South Node feels like an 'empty cup that needs to be filled'.

When looking at the North Node, the ruler of the node and aspects need to be considered as well as the house and sign position. As we delineate the axis of fate we need to ask: How do we balance these energies? How do we use the gifts of the South Node in the service of the North Node direction?

The Nodes progress 'backwards' through the chart, so we will consider their path starting with the 12th house and moving clockwise back to the first.

Planets transiting the nodes relate to the creation of karma. Venus, for example, will transit the nodes every year, but slower planets less often; Jupiter every 20 years, Saturn every 40 years. The slower planets are creating karma for future lives.

When an astrologer finds that a client does not resonate or relate to the indications of the MC, they should check the lunar nodes. Remember the South Node is always the comfort zone. These skills and gifts need to be integrated with the Sun and the MC and the North Node direction.

A square to the North Node can also show a profession. It is pointing to the qualities you are going to be forced to develop.

Where the North Node is transiting is where you have to improve to increase success.

North Node in the 12th House

The 12th, 11th and 10th houses make up the fourth quadrant of the natal chart. There is an association with teaching and learning.

The 12th house has memories of past lives and natives with this placement are able to download information from past eras.

There is also an awareness of the prenatal life. They remember the environment surrounding their mother while she was pregnant and what happened in the final month of pregnancy.

It is a spiritual house and most certainly contains 'buried treasure'. However, it can be difficult to integrate the energies and awareness in life.

12th house node natives (as well as 8th house ones) have to be reminded not to lose too much time in life 'licking their wounds'. The best response is to go out and help others with their wounds, it will cure one's own.

Vocations that pertain to this nodal position include welfare services, probation work, research, hypnosis, music, monastic life, dream analysis, astrology, marine-related professions, writing and poetry. Typical environments are hospitals, asylums and hostels for the homeless. It relates to foreign places, the 12th house describing places that are across oceans (and the 9th foreign places that do not entail crossing oceans).

Narrow down the possibilities by considering the sign placement. Cancer might more likely suggest the writing and poetry; Pisces the work with the suffering or under-privileged or perhaps the dream work; Capricorn is more likely drawn to a research role, something more concrete.

The Moon and the North Node are 'happy places': follow them whenever possible.

North Node in the 11th House

This placement can indicate a need to be famous. However, if the ruler of this house is at the bottom of the chart or in a secretive or shy sign, this is a contradiction to be resolved.

At any rate there is a need to engage with the community, to make connections and inspire others. With this 11th house node, you make your own 'family of choice'.

It can describe political or advisory jobs, or work within government or large institutions. As it is the 2nd from the 10th house, it could describe the native as an asset of the government.

The 11th house is also a house of friends, mentors and benefactors. The native must be sure to listen to these people—avoiding being stubborn like the Uranian /Aquarian nature of the house could suggest or indeed being too self-centred (reflecting the 5th house polarity house). The 11th house North Node native needs to think in terms of the good of the collective and never to consider themselves as superior in any way—in this arena all men are equal.

North Node in the 10ᵗʰ House

A Lunar North Node here at the MC, at the most elevated point of the chart indicates a native who needs to be out in the public arena. This is a huge challenge to the 4ᵗʰ house South Node. These individuals often struggle to balance work and family life and end up making sacrifices in one or the other.

They are destined for leadership, perhaps for stardom. Suitable work includes business ownership, entertainment, or acting. They need to forget the past and conquer their fear of publicity. The South Node position suggests that this will scare them. Paradoxically, as the North Node is a 'hungry point', it can also indicate a person who is obsessed with their career or with being in the spotlight.

Other associated work arenas are management in general, chiropractic therapy, coffee related businesses, and recycling services.
We need to consider any planets squaring the nodes in particular, they can suggest the spur or the hurdle to be overcome to conquer their reluctance.

Evolutionary astrologers designate planets in square to the nodes as 'skipped steps', life lessons we failed to learn in past incarnations and must revisit before we can move on in our soul journey.

South Node on the MC

This Nodal position speaks of obstacles to do with childhood experience. Frequently the parents are poor, uneducated or beset with serious problems. The individual does not develop much confidence or ambition. They may be haunted by the past or some sort of tragedy or trauma. The South Node is an intensely spiritual point. Natives with this placement are old souls.

North Node in the 9th House

This is the beginning of the 'Villain' Quadrant (7th, 8th and 9th houses). The individual with this placement needs a Big Vision. They need to explore what life can offer, perhaps operating in an international arena. It is the perfect position for the visionary or guru, for master teachers or writers.

Suitable careers are the import/export trade, public relations, marketing, philosophy or university-level teaching.

North Node in the 8ᵗʰ House

The challenge to the individual with this Lunar Node placement is to learn to share resources or, more challenging still, share their deepest secrets. This is particularly the case for natives with a diurnal chart. They have to learn to trust and overcome the internal script that says 'there is no help from others'. And at some level they are going to have to engage with money. They may have given much in past lives, the lesson of this life is to share, to give and receive, indeed to *expect* help from others. They should also use their sexuality or sexual charisma in some way in their career.

Suitable careers include: Financial Advisors or Planners, Insurance Underwriters, Venture Capitalists, Brokers and such roles involving collaboration and resources.

North Node in the 7th House

This is the first 'visible' experience house of the soul: You can consider the 6th as the house where you get dressed and prepare to meet the world, the 7th house is the threshold of the front door.

The 7th house describes unintegrated parts of the psyche. It represents, yes, other significant one-to-one relationships; people and partners. It is also where we discover ourselves through the mirror of relationships.

People with the North Node here usually experience hardship in this arena of close relationship in the early part of their lives. Some say this is the sequitur of selfishness in previous lives. They have to learn to take the risk required to engage fully in a relationship, to learn to live a symbiosis, how to give and take and how to compromise.

It suggests vocational roles such as negotiators, hosts, caterers, counsellors and people who work with contracts of any kind are suitable.

North Node in the 6ᵗʰ House

The importance of this placement is for the individual to be of service to humanity and to be very practical and organised in their approach. The South Node is in Pisces, they may wish to deal in spiritual matters or pursuits, but they should do this in a practical and useful manner, not just philosophically.

These natives should be working in contact with people where they are helpful to others. Probably they will be displaying some degree of selflessness in their role. They will display the Virgoan objectives, sorting, classifying or analysing, and then assimilating data, rather in the way the alimentary system absorbs food.

The ruler will show suitable roles or arenas of work for this placement. e.g., ruler in the 9ᵗʰ house: teaching, node in the 6ᵗʰ: in a practical way.

Taurus on the 6ᵗʰ cusp: subjects like food production or earth-related matters.

These natives are probably great at customer service and in general are problem solvers.

North Node in the 5th House

The native with this placement has to work in a way that engages their creative centre. They have to learn to be child-like and playful in their approach. It is probably better to be your own boss and work alone more than with others.

The 5th house is speculative and encourages risk taking. If there are other relevant correlations (8th house, 2nd house, Taurus, Scorpio) trading on the stock market could be suitable. In any event, with a 5th house North Node, you do not depend on the judgement of others. It remains important to the native, however, to be well regarded and accepted by the community.

North Node in the 4th House

The North Node here indicates a certain potential power. It is connected to roots and genetics. It is also highly influenced by mood, so it fluctuates to some degree.

The native needs to put down roots and will be drawn to work with land, farming, or real estate, perhaps in building or construction. Being involved in a family business is also likely.

As the fourth house also rules the 'end of the matter', so with a relevant other indicator (Scorpio or 8th house) this might suggest work in the funeral business.

North Node in the 3rd House

With the Node in this position, the native will be asked to communicate their own thoughts and ideas on everyday matters. They have to become a Master Communicator on a practical level of thought. This is very hard if the ruler is located in the 9th, this contrary pull means the native will struggle to reconcile the karmic axis.

Third house node position suggests a career in vocational training. Writing is indicated: short-length writing, lyric writing or screenplays. Social media is a possible suitable job—again assuming practical content.

North Node in the 2nd House

With the North Node in the 2nd house, the native needs to focus on using their own skills. They need to be making their own money and building their confidence and learning new skills. It is also very important to do work which reflects what you value. There can be some hesitation with asking for reasonable payment. They have to support themselves before supporting others and be more assertive. They are learning to trust their own instincts.

There can be anomalies in their attitudes to money. They may be greedy for money, hoard their earnings and refuse to spend it, getting themselves out of the cycle of spending and earning and renewing wealth. It is a classic position for careers like bankers, investors and stockbrokers.

North Node in the 1st House

This position for the North Node indicates a native whose life is very fated or predestined. They are going to be challenged to develop themselves in the course of a path of life that is very bumpy with steep learning curves. Sometimes they are strictly controlled in the early part of their lives. A major lesson for them is to concentrate on acting in their own interest, achieve for themselves and not to be drawn into advocating for others.

They are challenged to be extroverted and self-confident. Often, they are physically tall and lanky, although planets in square to the ascendant can influence this tendency.

Suitable careers are the military, sports and PE jobs, the type of sport will be shown by the sign and ruler. It is best for them to be self-employed.

South Node in the 1st House

Those with the South Node in the First are the archetypal old souls. They are interested in dualities and also in issues of fairness. They can tend to extremes. They are born to bring help and healing to others, releasing their persona and living for others. Early life can be extremely uncomfortable for them, some may fall prey to drug and addiction issues. They make great astrologers, occultists, scientists, designers and literary figures.

The Moon

The Moon needs must always be a priority. The Moon is what makes you happy. It also describes instinctual behaviours. It is essential that Moon needs are recognised and fulfilled, or else Moon misbehaves with unfortunate consequences. We need to look at the Moon, the Moon house placement as well as the Moon's ruler and its placement.

Moon placements tell us about family influences and emotional responses that can impact career progression or act as a block.

It can also be helpful to consider the 4th house cusp (the fourth being the Cancerian 'natural zodiac' lunar house).

Our moon describes our deepest needs. It shows what we need to feel secure, safe and to feel happy. We cannot ignore the Moon. If we don't give the Moon what it wants and needs, it will play up and kick off and generally cause mayhem either internally or externally.

The Moon is extremely important in vocational astrology therefore, we spend a huge chunk of our lives at work and the situation has to meet our lunar needs for happiness.

The sign and house placements should be examined.

Aries Moon

Aries Moon is the moon sign of the warrior. They want action, adventure and challenge—and they want it now. There is an impatience and an impulsiveness to the Aries Moon.

They are not necessarily angry. That would be the expression of an unintegrated and ignored Aries Moon. If they are being defensive, picking fights or acting in confrontational ways, that is born out of frustration and an environment that does not allow them to use their natural proclivities.

They have superb positive qualities: courage, enthusiasm, directness and a fierce loyalty, like that of 'brothers in arms'. Although sometimes charged with selfishness, the best Aries Moon is simply focused on what they need and how they can achieve it. They thrive on a challenge and love to pioneer a new idea, be the best or be first at something. They are natural innovators.

They need a work environment where they are 'given their head' and empowered to act and express their drive. This will inspire others around them.

Taurus Moon

The Taurus Moon wants a simple, peaceful life. What makes Taurus Moon happy is security (both mental and emotional), predictability and comfort. They will be steady, reliable and dependable which are sterling qualities in the workplace—but only if the workplace is steady and reliable for them.

They are more impressed by common sense and practicality than high blown ideas.

Food and sensual pleasures make Taurus Moon happy. Food-related careers might be indicated here. They don't have to impress others with any sort of fanciness. They want things to feel good and be solid and long-lasting, whether it's a relationship or a sofa. In fact, stuff is very important to them: Unless you really know it is okay, don't touch their stuff!

A connection to nature is important to them, so careers in a natural environment are very apt, perhaps as environmentalists, caring for animals, as farmers or as gardeners. Another resonance for Taurus Moon is music, which they may find soothing. They might even incline to singing as a career. Taurus is Venus ruled, so there is a creative side to Taurus Moon.

Taurus Moon will not like environments of unpredictability where they are under time pressure. When they seem overly materialistic, this is born of a need for security, not greed. They can be extraordinarily stubborn in the face of external pressure which makes them feel frazzled and overwhelmed. Only Cancer Moon is a better listener than Taurus Moon. They themselves are very self-reliant. Their grounded stability and earthy solidity can be helpful to colleagues. They give good hugs.

Gemini Moon

Gemini is all about communication, ideas and words. Moon is about the feeling realm. Gemini Moon needs to express feelings. It shows love by talking and feels nurtured and cared for by others when they talk with Gemini Moon.

What makes Gemini Moon happy, apart from talking, is learning. They are book-eaters and devour internet pages for breakfast and feel joy in gaining new knowledge. They are insatiably curious and everything interests them. Learning something new and sharing it and work that requires such activity, is the right arena for them. Like scientists, they explore and discover new things; they spot patterns and work out what is going on.

Playing with words delights them. Writing, speaking, wit, banter and amusing puns delight them.

Mercury also rules the hands, so manual crafts and skills might be suitable employment for Gemini Moon. Their ideal work has variety and lots of social interaction.

They will suffer in work situations that are repetitive and lack novelty or the opportunity to continually uncover new information.

Cancer Moon

The Cancer Moon is deeply soulful, sensitive and emotional. Cancer Moon operates and understands life in the realm of feeling. They embody the Great Mother archetype. They are very empathic and nurturing. The primary need is for emotional security and they are nurtured by nurturing others.

The main focus for Cancer Moon is typically home and family, but their innate skills are invaluable in the workplace too. They are excellent at caring roles, nursing, teaching young children, helping and supporting vulnerable people in all kinds of situations. Cancer Moon is kind and cares, and is the absolute best moon at listening to others. They make good counsellors, therapists and mentors. Looking after others makes Cancer Moon happy. They need to remember though that they are a cardinal moon and they need to take leadership in some way in their work.

This extreme sensitivity comes with the risk of their own emotional vulnerability. And a hurt Cancer Moon retreats into its shell and sometimes never truly comes out again. A Cancer Moon that has been damaged by harsh treatment or who works in an environment where they are not respected will be defensive and hang onto hurt and resent-ment (they do tend to hang onto things.) They can get lost or stuck in the past.

They are also subject to moods; their ruler the Moon waxes and wanes and moves swiftly from sign to sign and Cancer Moon resonates with all that.

Cancer Moon needs to be in touch with their emotional waves and accommodate them in their work schedule and practices. Taking a shower or changing their clothes when stressed are simple, effective Cancer Moon life hacks.

Cancer Moon is excellent in public facing roles such as in hospitality. They are personable, that hard to define but shiningly evident character trait, and intuitively respond to the emotional needs of others to feel comfortable and safe and 'at home'.

Leo Moon

This fiery moon has directness, honesty and strong loyalty. Leo Moon needs a stage of some sort and recognition as a leader. The best Leo Moons have regal qualities, they understand that The King is essentially the servant of the people and are ready to put the greater good or the needs of others foremost.

When the Leo Moon loses its way or finds itself in the wrong milieu, this is when they can appear arrogant or resort to manipulative or domineering behaviour; this usually comes from insecurity or being mocked or overlooked.

In the right environment, the Leo Moon shows its star quality. They have a natural charisma and presence. Another 18 carat feature of Leo Moon is their great generosity. They will like to show off a little in their personal presentation, through clothes and décor. What they need is to be seen and to be accorded respect and acknowledged for their leadership. In the right environment, they purr and play and are wonderfully affectionate and fun-loving: think of the lion family relaxing on the Savannah.

Virgo Moon

The mutable Virgo Moon needs things to be practical and tangible. They are not going to be impressed with fancy rhetoric, they need to see what works.

The Virgo imperative is not 'virginal' at all; Earth signs are all sensual in that sense. What Virgo moon needs is to be of service. Being Mercury ruled, Virgo Moon can be intrigued by many ideas and potential paths, but in this way their energy can be scattered. It is vital that the Virgo Moon focuses and chooses one or at most two paths(they are mutable after all). The key to career success for Virgo Moon is to become a master of their craft: above all other moon signs they are best placed to achieve this. Serving an apprenticeship of some sort is a typical Virgo Moon trajectory. Having a special skill that they can use to help others is ideal as they need to be needed. It is essential to their self-worth.

Virgo Moon is renowned for their critical faculties. Ill-expressed or under pressure this becomes hyper-criticism and 'nit-picking'. Virgo Moon applies this to themselves most of all. If they are too perfectionist and judgmental of themselves, they inhibit their success by making themselves feel hopeless and depressed. A well-prepared, experienced Virgo Moon at the top of their game can feel great pride in their offerings to others.

Most Virgo Moons will benefit from order in their environment and working practices. Cleanliness and tidiness are emotionally soothing to them and give a calming, functional environment. The house position of the Virgo Moon will indicate where the order is most essential.

They are detail-oriented and analytical, so dealing with data can suit them, as well as any complex organisational task. Ensuring standards in roles such as health and safety, hygiene or compliance work can be suitable, as long as they see the practical benefits.

The stressed or improperly integrated Virgo Moon, or a Virgo Moon in an unsuitable environment can exhibit 'control freak' behaviours. They should aim for strong self-control and attend to lunar needs to avoid this. They will be emotionally calm in an ordered environment where their contribution is practical and of service to others. They are happy if they can use their natural analytic skills for the betterment of others and the work setting.

Libra Moon

Fairness and harmonious relationships are what Libra Moon needs. They need to see fairness and justice, or work to make it happen. Libra, as an Air sign, is about connecting with others, and Libra Moon does so with grace, style and diplomacy. When other people are happy, Libra Moon is happy.

This Venusian Moon needs an environment that is in harmony and is peaceful in order to feel happy. It will probably help if it is aesthetically pleasing, too. They will enjoy working in arenas where they can use their charm and tact to bring peace and balance to situations and issues.

However, they need to be sure their desire for peace doesn't lead them to become 'people pleasers', denying their own rights or compromising too much. They are the sociable, famously lucky 'people who need people'.

Happy careers for Libra Moon are in PR, consulting, HR, diplomacy or other negotiating roles. Venus-ruled Libra Moon will also be content in the Fine Art arena, as a practitioner or in the allied industries. Fashion, Make-Up and Interior Design are other possibilities; the house position and other chart factors will help show where they can use their innate sense of harmony and balance.

Libra Moon will be wretched in noisy, combative or overly-competitive environments.

Scorpio Moon

Scorpio Moon is interested in power and power dynamics. They also have an intuitive sense of what motivates others. There is a forensic ability to work out what is going on below the surface of any situation.

They thrive on intensity and passion and can be comfortable in 'heavy' environments or dealing with taboo or psychologically challenging issues. They love crisis for breakfast. They do need their personal privacy, though. Scorpio Moon does not choose easily to reveal their turbulent emotions and they *all* have secrets. Their most impressive qualities are a great bedrock courage and an almost frightening level of willpower.

Good areas of work for them are psychology, policing and investigation, profiling, surgery and work to do with transformation and the power issues of sex, death and shared finance.

Trust issues are huge with Scorpio Moon. They need to be able to trust personal and work partners and truth and honesty are paramount. Scorpio Moon would always rather be hurt than lied to.

When Scorpio Moon is hurt, they can withdraw from everything and despair will take them to some dark places. However, they shine that penetrating psychological spotlight on themselves as much as on others and they are willing to do the work. They are brilliant at transforming, making themselves over and starting again from scratch. Scorpio Moon is a born survivor.

Sagittarius Moon

The mutable fire moon is concerned with natural justice and personal freedom. Sagittarius Moon needs to continually learn and expand their consciousness. They have to travel whether physically or intellectually. Other cultures inspire and intrigue them. A Sagittarius Moon needs a world stage—operating globally or drawing inspiration on a global scale. They are not about details or small gestures.

Sagittarius Moon either has the soul of a scholar or the soul of a gypsy (in the world-traveller sense). They also have the fire qualities of instinct and intuition and need to be able to tune into that and use it wisely. They are born philosophers. They want to know what it is all about and why we are here. They need work that touches on this and illuminates this in some way. In a nutshell, their life and their work must have 'meaning'. There is a lot of courage there too. The emotional courage of Sagittarius Moon is quite moving, they 'bounce back' (there is a Jupiterian image) from hurt and disappointment, bravely blink away the tears and carry on.

They are out of balance when bogged down in the small stuff or if they feel restricted. They can then overcompensate, start to impose their own ideas and get carried away or over-confident about a project or idea. Something is off when they start to evangelise or close off to the ideas and input of others. They need to keep their feet on the ground and remember they are here to discover truth and stand for natural justice.

They are the world's natural teachers and are here to inspire others and share their knowledge. Any organisation will benefit from their optimism and vision of future possibilities. Someone else will have to fact-check and take care of the details, though! At a gathering, you will find them deep in discussion on the meaning of life, probably not helping with the washing up.

Capricorn Moon

Moon in Capricorn is one of the toughest placements. These people are here to achieve. They need to do this with integrity and by assuming responsibility, not to mention hard work. What makes Capricorn Moon happy is moving up the tree and being recognised for that achievement. They have a need to build a reputation and leave a legacy. Pride in what they have built is their best reward, better than money. The house position of Capricorn Moon will give insight into where they need to have a visible and substantial achievement. For instance, a fourth house Capricorn Moon would find fulfilment in building a house, perhaps a fifth house Capricorn Moon might need to paint a masterpiece or have some other significant creative expression.

Capricorn Moon must find time to be alone, to be a hermit for a while, although they may feel guilty or sad about being away from family for that time. Looking within, they must find a way to believe they are good and worthy. Whatever happened in this or a previous lifetime where they fell short, this is the lifetime to become a master and 'boss up'.

On a personal level, Capricorn Moon, with its inner demons of loneliness and unworthiness, is healed when they realise no one has to earn love, not them, not the others around them. To love and be loved is a birthright.

Aquarius Moon

Aquarius Moon people are famous for their emotional detachment. It is not that they don't have emotions, of course they do, but they are not happy expressing them freely. They try to process emotion intellectually and logically, and emotions don't work in that way.

What matters to Aquarius Moon is freedom. This can be a barrier in the personal arena when they refuse a relationship they would enjoy in the name of freedom. One of their best features is their friendliness. They tend to have lots of friends and to appreciate them. Once they do form a bond with someone, they are loyal with all the fixity of a fixed sign.

What makes the Aquarius Moon happy is changing the world to be a better place. Aquarius Moon has seen the future and they have a keen sense of social justice. They are fulfilled working for the betterment of humanity. Fighting for change: equality, human rights and fair access to resources and opportunities are ideal occupations. They need to be allowed to do things in their own way and to make their own systems. They will find it hard to follow and recipe, and will have to tweak and innovate. They are all inventors in some way or other.

It is vital for them to find an outlet for their genius. Technology, IT, cybernetics and any new and unusual field is a good place for Aquarius Moon. These folks are often very bright.

They need to gravitate to environments where their uniqueness and unconventionality is appreciated and understood. They enjoy the company of others who are as unconventional and individual as they are. An unintegrated Aquarius Moon or one trying to operate in the wrong job environment risks being cast into the role of black sheep or shunned outsider. They don't belong in rigid, traditional work situations and they should not try to fit in with one. They do operate well in groups and communities and they understand the power of collaboration and group action.

Aquarius Moon has a rebellious soul. There is the fixed sign tendency to stubbornness, perhaps a fault and perhaps just Aquarius Moon sticking to their guns because they understand what the rest of us mere mortals have not yet understood.

Pisces Moon

Pisces Moon people are compassionate, imaginative, intuitive (even psychic) individuals in touch with the realms of magic and deeply connected to the universe and 'All That Is'. They can seem a little other-worldly, naïve or vague. Pisces Moon truly understands how we are all connected to each other and all life in the world, and are here to fathom the mysteries of the universe.

They have such sensitivity they need to have access to peaceful and natural environments. They need to retreat often to recharge their batteries, taking frequent holidays, even if short ones. They need to set up homes that are sanctuaries from a harsh world. They lack the boundaries to operate in toxic environments and can be quickly drained of energy by other people. They also take longer to recover physically, psychologically and emotionally from negative experiences.

Their powerful imaginations fit them for artistic and creative careers. They are often drawn to the ocean, and marine-related careers are also suitable paths for them. They want to save people, sometimes even those who don't want to be saved, and can fall into 'victim-saviour-persecutor' psychological drama triangles. They may well be drawn to work with the most vulnerable in society, the homeless, prisoners, refugees and abuse survivors or those challenged by drug and alcohol addiction. They incline and attune to the spiritual and may find themselves living in monasteries or pursuing a spiritual quest. They will need to relate to the spiritual meaning behind whatever work they do.

Compassion and kindness are the strongest tools available to humanity and Pisces Moon can achieve great good in the world. A healthy Pisces Moon also has an extraordinary desire and ability to forgive, which is powerfully healing in so many situations.

Using the Zenith Point

Whereas the MC is a point in the sky relating to the 'midday' of the chart, the zenith is subtly different. It is a point 90° above the ascendant or horizon point. The zenith is reflective of psychological motivations underpinning what we choose to do. We need to look at both MC and zenith perspectives.

For example, imagine a Pisces MC, in the third decan—that is Pisces with a Scorpionic quality. The Sun is Aquarius, again third decan, so with a Libra quality. Moon is Pisces too, but second decan, so with a Cancerian influence. IC is Virgo, with a third decan/Taurean quality. This suggests a healing (Pisces) career but with a Scorpionic flavour, so forensic, psychological and deep. The Sun is Aquarian, so futuristic, humanitarian and idealistic in mission, in the third decan, with a Libra flavour, so approach could be to work in partnership or to seek harmony and grace in communications and collaborations. Pisces Moon needs are in keeping with the MC indications and suggest a caring or nurturing quality to the work is necessary to happiness and fulfilment.

The zenith is in Aries. The blend of MC (Pisces) and Zenith (Aries) energies is difficult: fire and water are incompatible. Fire evaporates water and water puts out fire. The native might have a conscious desire to pursue a healing career, but the subconscious zenith imperative is to lead, come first, be a pioneer and 'do it her way' in a driven and active way. These incompatible MC and zenith energies illustrate an advanced technique for understanding what could be blocking career success.

When looking at the zenith a 3° orb is appropriate. Hard aspects: squares, oppositions, quincunxes to planets, fixed stars and asteroids are significant and illuminate other potential career blockages.

Fixed Stars

We consider the influence of a fixed star when it conjuncts the Sun, Moon, North Node or an angle, career planet or angle ruler. There is a maximum orb of two degrees. There are many fixed stars, but it is really the 15 'Behenian Stars' that count: these are the stars considered by mediaeval European and Arab scholars to have the most astrological power. The word 'Behenian' derives from the Arabic for 'root'.

Degree	Star	Nature	Notes
26 Taurus 26	Alghol	Saturn & Jupiter	Malefic star; positively can confer power-but then you lose it
0 Gemini 16	Alcyone/ Pleiades	Moon & Mars	
10 Gemini 04	Aldebaran	Mars & Venus	A star of popularity (including social media fame) Another royal star. Association with Archangel Michael. Royal Star
22 Gemini 08	Capella	Jupiter & Saturn	
14 Cancer 21	Sirus	Venus	
26 Cancer 03	Procyon	Mercury & Mars	
0 Virgo 06	Regulus	Jupiter & Jupiter	Royal Star
27 Virgo 12	Alkaid	Venus & Moon	
13 Libra 43	Algorab	Saturn & Mars	

Degree	Star	Nature	Notes
24 Libra 06	**Spica**	Venus & Mercury	
24 Libra 30	**Arcturus**	Mars & Jupiter	
12 Scorpio 34	**Alphecca**	Venus & Mars	
10 Sagittarius 01	**Antares**	Venus & Jupiter	Gives access to secrets Extra-ordinary ability to create / manifest. Royal Star
15 Capricorn 34	**Vega**	Mercury & Venus	
23 Aquarius 48	**Deneb Algedi**	Saturn & Mercury	

Also significant are:

Fomalhaut (4 Pisces) is associated with Magic and Astrology. It brings fame at a late age. (Always a need for careful, compassionate use of spiritual knowledge if used for gain). It is the fourth Royal Star.

Rigel (16 Gemini) is the star of the entrepreneur

Pollux (25 Cancer) is associated with the occult and a penetrating mind.

Asteroids and Centaurs

The centaur Chiron and the asteroid Hygeia relate to healing and healing ability in the chart. Of the major asteroids, Pallas Athena, Juno and Ceres are the most pertinent to vocational considerations. Most of the planets were named for masculine mythological figures except Venus; the Moon relates to feminine principles but the luminaries are really 'beyond gender'. The asteroids however relate to feminine archetypes. They were discovered and integrated into astrological understanding in parallel with women's emancipation, women's liberation and the reassertion of women's rights in society. In both women's and men's charts they add insight and balance. We use a maximum orb of 2°. In vocational analysis when using asteroids we are interested in aspects to the angles, the luminaries (Sun and Moon) and significant career planets, also aspects to rulers of the angles.

Chiron

Chiron is one of the centaurs, the most just and wise of the centaurs. Centaurs are half man and half horse (so associated with Sagittarius— the first 15 degrees of Sagittarius are considered animalistic, the second 15 degrees human). He was the son of the Titan Cronus or Saturn. So, Chiron is the son of Saturn, part man and part horse, but civilised, humanitarian, compassionate and healing.

Chiron was gravely wounded, but being immortal, did not die and remained in endless pain. He was gifted with the ability to heal others, but not himself. Eventually he gave up his immortality and was killed by Heracles with a poisoned arrow. It was Chiron, a powerful healer who taught healing to Asclepius, the God of Medicine.

Astronomically, Chiron orbits between Saturn, the last visible planet, and Uranus, the first invisible planet, reflecting Chiron's ability to see the past and the future. He heals what is between the visible and the invisible (as what Barbara Hand Clow called the 'Rainbow Bridge').

Chiron is the 'wounded healer'. It speaks of victimisation and also of the saviour. Consider Chiron in a chart and ask where we make excuses for our failures and where we might even be creating our own wounds. Nonetheless this is the area where we can heal others.

Chiron and the aspects made to it in our birth chart could illuminate blockages to career and success.

Sun-Chiron

Chiron in aspect to the Sun is very like the Sun-Saturn aspect. There is often a strongly authoritarian parent. There is a fear of going for what one wants in life. It's safer not to have goals, better not to start than to risk failure. They either never start projects or won't let them go until perfect.

With Chiron-Sun there is a fear of living, a fear of 'shining', a fear of outshining a father or partner. Sometimes they end up stepping into their father's shoes—where they are miserable and not appreciated.

Often there is a lot of responsibility carried at a very early age, the child never feels good enough and becomes over-responsible and perfectionist.

Moon-Chiron

Classic signature of a mother who is an ice queen or emotionally distant (or absent, or dead).

There is no real family bond and this person works to create a family. It is the Moon of the struggling lone parent, for instance. It's a Moon that fears people in general. They need to focus on nurturing skills and on being nurtured. They should strive to overcome emotional distance.

The Moon should reflect the Sun, but this Moon is scared to reflect her Sun and shine. This Moon is not allowed to guide her to her goals in life. They can't get positive feedback and fear promotion.

The Moon is moody and this person can set themselves up for failure, unpopularity and blame. They are often anxious and depressed. All Moon-Chiron aspects are difficult. The sextiles and trines are easier to fix.

Mercury-Chiron

With Mercury-Chiron the wound is to the intellect or thinking. These individuals may find it difficult to speak up; there might be a language barrier or speech impediment. The person might feel that no-one would want to hear their opinions or be paralysed by fear of making a mistake; there might have been rules around 'permission to speak' in the family background. This aspect can also manifest as difficult energies in sibling relationships. Individuals with this signature might have been ridiculed for some aspect of their speech or expression. The healing journey is to honour your voice and perhaps to empower others to find theirs or perhaps to act as an advocate for the voiceless.

Venus-Chiron

The Venus-Chiron wound is to the self-worth. People with this aspect may be too scared to do what they would enjoy doing. Perhaps they feel they don't deserve happiness or that joy and fun are in some way forbidden for them. Sometimes there are limiting beliefs that only certain ways of making a living are acceptable.

This Chiron wound can be expressed as difficulty with money, and having programmed ideas that restrict a healthy relationship to money.

It could even be that the actuality of being a woman is perceived as a barrier to success, achievement, and pursuing happiness. With Venus-Chiron aspects one can be inhibited to express their sexiness or have strange ideas about certain clothes or aspects of the appearance that they consider not respectable, acceptable or attractive.

Sadly, some Venus-Chiron people believe deep down that love has to be earned, when it is of course their birth right to love and be loved as much as anyone else. Love does not have to be hard work as they might think. They might have experiences of their personal relationships blocking their career, through the healing of the Venus-Chiron wound they find ways to break down these barriers.

Mars-Chiron

Mars-Chiron aspects lead an individual to be acutely aware of their limitations and to lack bravery or the desire to compete. Perhaps they might think "I'm second best, so why even try?" They will not honour their feelings by changing course or giving up on an activity that does not serve them, they trudge on regardless. They cannot stand up for themselves and are overly compliant with others' rules and expectations.

It is an aspect that can be associated with any sort of abuse. Certainly, there is a deep subconscious wound. This can play out in a person's career with no one understanding the origin of the problem. Another expression of Mars-Chiron is a low energy level. In a man's chart it can indicate impotency.

Mars-Chiron individuals often feel compelled to help others, but don't allow themselves to be selfish or to follow their dreams.

Jupiter-Chiron

With Jupiter-Chiron there can be a wound around belief systems. Often there is a strictly religious or normative upbringing. There can be a religious problem, or moral codes or dogmas can impede the native from succeeding. The problem arises from a perceived lack of meaning. This can lead to a very negative or pessimistic outlook.

Possible expressions of the Jupiter-Chiron energy are being rigidly materialist, not believing in anything beyond the tangible ("Seeing is believing"). These natives don't allow themselves to dream or to be optimistic. Sometimes they refuse to aspire towards abundance in life. There can be an exaggerated fear of karmic outcomes ("What goes around, comes around").

It might even manifest as a fear of flying.

Saturn-Chiron

People with Saturn-Chiron aspects can have a deeply depressive and negative outlook. They are blocked from rising to positions of authority. It could be that actual superiors are standing in their way. They can also be limited by a lack of belief in their capabilities that leads them to avoid opportunities for promotion, although they deeply desire it.

They may be adversely affected by the influence of a father figure, who undermined their self-belief.

In general, they are limited by fears, of failure, of responsibility; of growing up at all. This can lead to them appearing very rigid in front of others.

Together with the aura of negativity, apparent lack of ambition and a tendency to be stuck in the past, they do not fit themselves for success.

Uranus-Chiron

People with a Chiron-Uranus aspect are not able to embrace their uniqueness. They fear appearing eccentric or standing out from the crowd. They don't want to be the 'black sheep' or not fit in. They worry others won't like them if they show their real selves.

Rules and regulations infuriate them, but they can't bring themselves to break the rules. They will agree to follow orders, but subvert them by doing things a little bit differently. They irritably find other people stupid.

They can have a fear of the future, it's a scary place for Uranus-Chiron.

Neptune-Chiron

The Neptune-Chiron person has wounds around the Neptunian and Pisces realms. Frequently there is a guilt around pursuing or attaining success.

They might feel they must show compassion in order to be noticed and find success, rather than just embracing compassion as a laudable approach to people.

They fear chaos and exploring their own imagination and creativity. Vague people annoy them because they are in touch with the energies which they themselves fear. They are prey to conspiracy theories, too prone to believe they are being betrayed and inclined to blame others for their failures and misfortunes. Their victim mentality may stem from a family background of well-hidden problems or dictatorial parents who impose what they think is best for the individual. The world is a tough place where they feel they don't belong.

Pluto-Chiron

For the Pluto-Chiron person the wound is around power and control. The individual experiences powerlessness and either feels hopeless or reacts by becoming controlling themselves. They are overly bossy, and won't allow any contradiction or negotiation, seizing opportunities for the power they have been denied. Conversely, they may fear assuming leadership and fall into paranoia, thinking everyone is 'out to get them'. They may find it impossible to find their true life passion. They are born survivors, but are defensive and negative in approach. A typical idea is that life is an unending and extreme struggle and that they must work to the bitter end of it.

Sedna

The asteroid Sedna can be useful in identifying blockages to career success. This asteroid was discovered in 2003. Sedna has an elliptical orbit and spends 100 years in a sign: it was in Aries from 1865 to 1966. It is named for the Inuit goddess of the sea and marine animals.

There are various versions of the Sedna myth. One tells of a spoiled girl who turns down all suitors; eventually her father sells her to a hunter for a bucket of fish, but the man turns out to be a bird (a Fulmar) in disguise; in another she marries a dog and angers her father; in another she attacks her parents. In all versions she ends up out on the sea with her father in a kayak. He tries to throw her out and when she clings to the side, he cuts off her fingers. These severed fingers become the whales, dolphins and creatures of the deep. Sedna becomes an immortal sea goddess and sits at the bottom of the sea brooding and resentful with her long hair tangling about her. She has the power to control the sea animals (who are tangled in her hair).

The Inuit believed they had to appease and placate the vengeful Sedna in order to ensure successful hunting. Their shamans could travel in trance to the bottom of the sea and comb her tangled hair to soothe her and gain her help for the hunt.

In astrology, a prominent Sedna can indicate Father-Daughter problems. It can also relate to wrong marriages or ones where the partner changes after marriage. In some versions of the myth, Sedna is raped by a crow and so a significantly placed Sedna can relate to experience of rape.

It is a female energy and relates to suffragettes, struggles for female emancipation and female rage. The transition of Sedna into Taurus correlated with the bra-burning movement.

Sedna can resonate with Plutonian issues, betrayal, corruption, global-warming, and making money through drugs and sexual exploitation. It also has a Neptunian flavour and with a prominent Sedna, the individual can get caught up in the classic victim-saviour-persecutor triangle. Her orbit is between Pluto and Neptune (Sedna is a 'trans-Neptunian' object).

A prominent Sedna can suggest a troubled path, but once the true path is found, there is joy and peace in following the heart's desire—like when Sedna becomes a mermaid or sea goddess.

Sedna-inspired occupations include marine careers, spirituality, any ocean related work or family constellations work.

Hygeia

Hygeia was discovered in 1849. This asteroid is associated with preventative medicine and hygiene in general. Anything you do to promote wellbeing: breathing deep and staying hydrated and getting sufficient sleep are her preserve. As is sanitising, washing hands and brushing teeth, practices that control disease. She is forward thinking, hence the emphasis on prevention.

In mythology, Hygeia's father, Asclepius, was a pupil of Chiron who became known as the God of Medicine. His symbol is the Caduceus, the staff of Hermes with the entwined snakes. This is now the symbol for the World Health Organisation. Hygeia is also associated and depicted with snakes.

Snakes have an acute sensitivity—they feel the vibrations in the earth as they have their bellies to the ground.

Hygeia might be prominent in the chart of someone who works in environmental health, of a cleaner, a sanitation worker or someone who handles dead bodies, a vital public health role. It might also indicate a person who works to help with mental illness by promoting emotional and spiritual balance—perhaps in that way an astrologer has a place here.

Chiron is more about spiritual healing, Hygeia more about medical healing, but can be considered hand-in-hand. There is a similar theme of having to heal oneself before attempting to heal others.

Pallas Athena

Pallas Athena was the daughter of Zeus (also called Jupiter) and Metis. She was born from the head of Zeus after he swallowed Metis while she was pregnant. She was born fully grown and dressed in armour, carrying a sword and a shield. Pallas was Zeus' favourite daughter, although they fought fiercely. She was determinedly independent and never married. She did have a child, but by a sort of immaculate conception.

Among the Pallas myths is how she created the monster or gorgon Medusa. In a fit of jealousy she turned Medusa's hair into snakes and caused anyone Medusa looked upon to be turned to stone. Medusa had claimed to be more beautiful than Athena and Athena despised her for being frivolous and flirtatious in a way that was not appropriate for a temple guardian.

Pallas also fell out with Neptune. When she offered the people of a besieged city an olive branch, meaning to provide them with food and firewood, Neptune offered them the springtime and the people preferred his gift. In the way of Greek Gods and Goddesses, she sought revenge.

Being born from the head of Zeus relates to her association with intellect, prudence and cleverness. As a fighter, she used less brute force and more strategy; she would fight if she had to, but preferred to negotiate and reach an agreement if possible. She was also very much a champion of justice and thus is associated with all things legal.

A prominent Pallas in the chart suggests a clever sort of person who is likely to gravitate to 'Air sign' career choices. We associate Pallas with the signs Aquarius, Libra and Virgo particularly. Any work emphasising strategic thinking or planning is apt for someone with a prominent Pallas. They can spot trends and patterns and excel in analytics; this suits the Pallas influenced individual for 11th house related careers where spotting future trends and such skills are paramount. They might be involved in a fight for justice or equality or act as an advocate or champion for others. In any chart, the house where Pallas is located is a place where one might find oneself standing up and acting as an advocate; one will have a good holistic view of this area of life too.

Given her very close ties to Zeus, Pallas can highlight the father-daughter relationship for good or ill. Her symbolic armour could suggest a career where one makes or wears some sort of personal protective equipment Pallas can be prominent when there are fertility problems or this might indicate a career specialism in such issues.

There can be a certain loneliness or isolation with a strong Pallas, but these natives have fortitude and courage too.

The glyph for Pallas Athena is a grand cross above a cross of matter (meaning matter as the material realm). With a strong Pallas the individual will face big challenges in life, but if they focus on getting work dealing with what is important to them, and have the patience for the time it will take, they can overcome their difficulties. They can make money from work they truly enjoy or perhaps from a hobby. Any typically feminine industry is indicated too.

In a man's chart, a prominent Pallas can indicate a powerful wife or a life where they find themselves surrounded by women.

Vesta

Vesta (also called Hestia) was a Roman Vestal Virgin, one of the women chosen to safeguard the sacred flame in the temple, which was believed to protect the city and the army. Vestal virgins were chosen when they were children. Between the ages of 10 and 40 they devoted themselves utterly to their sacred duty.

Vesta was the oldest sister of Saturn (Chronos). The asteroid Vesta has an orbit of 3.62 years. Interestingly, when a person has their Saturn return, they also have their Vesta return. These are two indications of a Saturnian quality in Vesta.

The Vestal Virgins could not marry until after forty, when they were released from their responsibilities and granted the means for independent living for life, a huge pay-off for their services. Often people with a strong Vesta placement will come into their own after the age of forty. There is an association with independence from men and also of purity, devotion to duty and sacrifice for a higher cause.

With a prominent Vesta influencing vocation, there may be sacrifice required to achieve career success, as well as dedication and single-minded focus. Work could entail a degree of solitude or the individual might have a primarily spiritual existence in this incarnation.

Paradoxically, there is also an association with sexuality. Scholars believe the Vestal virgins were not technically virgins or chaste, but independent and not belonging to any man. They might have practised a sort of sacred sexuality. A strong Vesta might indicate a career as a nun, a sexual therapist or a prostitute, given the contradictory qualities of purity and passion.

The Vestals were chosen by Pontifex Maximus, a man they cherished. So sometimes, a strong Vesta shows a strong devoted connection to a boss.

The fire symbolism speaks of purifying and sterilising qualities, in the way fire is used to cauterise a wound. Vesta associated with vocation can therefore point to healing careers. Fiery Vesta is creative, so it might indicate ceramics, glass making or pyrography; art forms that require fire.

The childlessness of Vesta can point to working with infertility in some way.

If a Vestal touched a criminal by accident, they were forgiven their transgression, so Vesta is associated with healing touch, so a practice like Reiki, a spiritual healing touch therapy, could apply.

The Vestals also held wills and papers relating to the city, so someone with a prominent Vesta might work with similarly important documents.

Ceres

Ceres (or Demeter) is the goddess of grain and the harvest. In her myth, her beloved daughter Persephone was abducted by Pluto and carried off to the underworld. Such was her loss and grief as a mother, Ceres was consumed by rage. In her anger, she stopped the harvest and famine ensued. With the intercession of Mercury (or Hermes) and Jupiter (Zeus), Ceres was persuaded to come to an accommodation with Pluto. Her daughter was returned to her for half the year and for the rest of the year Persephone returned to Pluto. This is the myth of how the seasons came into being: growth and plenty in the spring and summer and dying back and dormancy in the autumn and winter.

Ceres is related to the relationships of mothers and daughters, and to mothers in general. It is also associated with excessive emotion and possessiveness. Wherever Ceres is in the chart is somewhere we experience highs and lows. When Ceres was discovered, it was conjunct the malefic fixed star Algol which has connection with beheading, so Ceres connects with 'losing one's head' with overwrought emotions.

A strong Ceres connection to career could indicate work to do with agriculture, horticulture and all aspects of food. It also relates to working with children or dealing with matters of family, also traditions, DNA or even past lives.

Ceres carries a watery and emotional energy and also resonances of the underworld. The related sign energies are Cancer, Scorpio and Pisces.

Anything to do with underground water-like springs or sewerage could feature in the career, as might caves, mines or other underground areas. There is a connection with animals, especially farm animals and in particular, bees.

Sadly, a strong Ceres could relate to child-loss by abduction, estrangement, death or miscarriage. Oddly, around the time Ceres was promoted to dwarf planet status from her original asteroid status, there were many publicised abductions, including that of Madeleine McCann.

With the connection to grief and rage, a strong Ceres is frequently seen in cases of serious depression. There is a need to find a way to move through the grief and rage and find happiness and fulfilment. A vocational connection to Ceres could suggest working with depression as a career, counselling people on how to cope with experiences of tragic loss.

Another career expression of a strong Ceres reflects her determination to protect her daughter, so security services might be a valid expression.

Day of Birth

The days of the week are named for the planets, so it is fun to check the day to give another career planet to focus on:

Monday	Moon
Tuesday	Mars
Wednesday	Mercury
Thursday	Jupiter
Friday	Venus
Saturday	Saturn
Sunday	Sun

You can consider the hour of birth too and the ruler of the hour. This gives an indication of karmic memory, something of the spirit the native came in with. These are minor considerations, but can add nuance to the career profile.

The Saturn Jupiter Cycle/Phases

The phases and cycle of Saturn and Jupiter in a personal horoscope gives information about the career life both in terms of the natal Saturn-Jupiter Phase and also by transit. (They are also highly significant in business and financial astrology).

Saturn is important because it gives indication of our attitude toward, and style of working; it can show the sort of work we choose and the methods we employ. The house placement of Saturn can give another flavour to the style.

Jupiter is the planet of expansion, luck and optimism and shows where life's gifts and opportunities are coming from.

Following a conjunction of Saturn and Jupiter (the 'Great Conjunction' which typically coincides with significant societal, political and economic change), Jupiter, the faster moving planet, will gradually distance itself from Saturn, separating ever further until at 20 years approximately it comes round to form another conjunction.

During the cycle, the two planets will pass through 8 major phase relationships in a similar way to the Moon Phases in the lunar cycle. The conjunction brings a New Moon Phase, followed by a Waxing Crescent, a First Quarter Square phase, a Waxing Gibbous phase, a Full Moon phase and Waning Gibbous phase, a Last Quarter Square phase and finally a Waning Crescent phase, culminating in a new conjunction.

Following a ('Great') conjunction of Saturn and Jupiter, the cycle of the two planets commences with a New Moon Phase when there are from 0-45 degrees between them. Natives born in a Saturn Jupiter New Moon phase are typically innovators who show a high level of ingenuity and thrive on challenges. They are independent, can be self-centered and use their strong intuition. They are suited to being 'in at the beginning' of new things: ideas, initiatives, businesses and developments in industry. They also thrive in self-employment.

This phase by transit brings a release from restrictions and burdens, new beginnings and a 'clean slate'.

In the next Saturn-Jupiter phase (from 45-90 degrees, the Waxing Crescent Phase) we have natives whose work life consists of challenges and obstacles to be overcome. If their work doesn't give these native obstacles, they create them themselves. They can find themselves wearing many hats and struggling with lots of details.

This phase by transit brings challenges like funding, paperwork and documentation overload, logistic and timetabling issues and the need to establish new protocols and routines.

Native born with the First Quarter Square Phase aspect between Saturn and Jupiter (90-135 degree separation) have strong management ability. They are the individuals who impose structure, rules and frameworks. They are motivated and identify and communicate clear targets and objectives. As they do this, they can incite crises in the workplace and may struggle with others resisting the structures they impose, although they are crucial to the development of the work project.

This aspect by transit is often experienced by lots of hours being put in, establishing crucial systems and 're-inventing wheels'.

The next Saturn-Jupiter phase is the Waxing Gibbous phase (135-180 degree separation). Natives here are looking for meaning in their work and for the opportunity to influence and inspire others by what they do. It is something of a 'ninth house' energy type aspect. They are looking for a philosophy underpinning their work and to understand its purpose.

Experienced by transit, this aspect finds people keen to do something different and to do it with others.

Native born at the Full Moon Phase between Saturn and Jupiter (180-225 degrees) find themselves experiencing constant stress at work. Sometimes the work is literally dangerous—this is the placement for firefighters, parachutists and similar professions. These people often find themselves highly visible through their work (even if just by their distinctive uniforms) and find themselves going to extremes in their careers.

This is a Full Moon phase and by transit people will often experience the necessity of giving up or letting go of something in the work sphere.

The Disseminating Phase (225-270 degrees) of the Saturn-Jupiter cycle is the placement for life's communicators and distributors. Suitable careers include the opportunity to write, teach, consult and disseminate. They identify key information, goods and ideas and get it out there. News and transportation are relevant fields.

By transit, people find themselves focusing on something of value and desirous to share it with the world, be it a product or a certain vision. In their enthusiasm they can come on too strong and appear overly pushy.

The Last Quarter Square Phase between Saturn and Jupiter natally (270-315 degrees separation) encounters challenges at work too. They are constantly trying to learn new skills to augment their career and have an interest in social reform and other ways of restructuring their world. Things are difficult for them if they do not manage to decide on their priorities and remain focused. They will be changed, so if the natal pattern involved fixed energies particularly, this could be hard to navigate. By transit this phase brings the desire to learn something new and upgrade their work. The person may be feeling dissatisfied, even if those around them value their contributions.

The Balsamic Phase (315-360 degrees) relationship between Saturn and Jupiter gives us natives with a more retiring nature and internal focus.

These people are very private individuals. They prefer to work behind the scenes and when they do, tend to a creative and artistic expression. They can feel uncertain about the future and be daunted and unclear as to how to proceed. These people make great researchers, coaches and personal assistants.

Then the planets proceed to another conjunction/New Moon Phase.

Saturn and Jupiter between them rule the last four zodiac signs and relate especially to humanity, society, universal laws and collective experience.

They come together every twenty years in the same element or tri-plicity. When this activates a particular house in a natal chart it shows an area of life with a strong potential for growth and achievement—but always at the cost of hard work and discipline.

Every two hundred years Saturn and Jupiter progress to a new tri-plicity. Every eight hundred years they have traversed all the elements.

Every sixty years Saturn and Jupiter reunite in the same sign and these conjunctions tend to coincide with societal and political shifts—the rise and fall of kings and presidents, as well as political regimes and empires.

You may see reference to their 'true conjunction' when the planets actually align in the sky and the 'mean conjunction' which occurs at very regular intervals and is calculated from the average motion of each planet.

Between 1842 and 2020, Saturn and Jupiter met in Earth signs (grounded, material) and we had a global earth economy. In Taurus, money was the key focus, and economic attitudes were headstrong, if slow moving. In Virgo we saw a focus on health issues, greater precision and analysis and a tendency to create tighter economic controls. In Capricorn we see the primacy of business corporations and a maturity of approach.

When the conjunctions move into Air from 2020 on, we will change to an 'Air economy' which has a more intellectual nature.

From 2020-2040 the planets will meet in Aquarius. This energy is revolutionary and concerned with humanitarian issues, equality and social justice.

From 2040 to 2060 they will meet in Libra which will bring a focus on relationship, balance and justice.

From 2060-2080 they will meet in Gemini and the economic priori-ties will relate especially to communications.

From 1980 to 2000 we had a 'preview' of the air economy and this saw the innovations of the web browser and the internet.

It is interesting to consider the last Air economy that pertained from 1226 to 1425 (with the 'preview' from 1186 to 1206). This era saw developments and expansion in education and exploration as well as technologies like printing and optics. There were political reforms like the Magna Carta and introduction of electoral colleges. Astrology saw a strong period including the contributions of Bonatti and the development of weather forecasting with astrology.

Areas that are set to expand and flourish in our new air age are:

Biotechnology

Communications Air purification Online learning Health diagnostics

Understanding of the brain

Wind power

Software

New ways of working and managing staff / HR

Analysing Aspects Pertaining to the Vocational Profile

Analysing an aspect goes beyond the simplistic 'good' and 'bad' designation of conjunctions, squares, oppositions, trines and sextiles.

First of all, we need to determine if the aspect is applying or separating, because this gives the aspect very different meanings.

When a faster moving planet closes up on a slower moving planet, the aspect is **applying**; when a faster moving planet increasingly distances itself from a slower moving planet, the aspect is **separating**. Thus, it is key to be aware of planetary speeds and any recent or upcoming retrograde that might alter the aspect.

An applying aspect speaks of the future and will be a continuous theme in life. A separating aspect speaks of an influence from the past, or previous lives possibly and its impact will likely diminish over the lifetime.

Keywords and concepts for Applying aspects:
Initial fumbling
Pending
The main event
To come
Pressure building
Future expectation

And for Separating aspects:
Knowing
Time for a nap
Early life theme
Pertaining to glory days
Fading

Exact (Partile) Aspects:

Exquisite
Perfect
Together
Ultimate

Unaspected Planets are interesting:

They can go two ways, either showing themselves as the purest expression of that planetary energy or expressing negatively and in a way that fails to integrate with the other chart energies expressing in life.

The Character of the Angles

Always first check the modes of the angles.

Mutable signs are about curiosity, change and busy-ness. This can make the person scattered. They may change jobs frequently. They get bored.

The Fixed modality is about security and stability. They stick with things, like routine and can be stubborn.

Cardinal signs on angles indicate an outlook of inspiration, challenge and driving ahead. They deal with the big issues.

Then check to see if the Ascendant/Descendant and Midheaven /IC are in harmony; also, if the angle modes relate to the personal planets. If they are jarringly different, for example a fixed Sun sign and mutable angles, this can be a difficult conflict of energies. An aspect between the rulers can indicate a path to resolution. An aspect between angle rulers will be a key aspect for analysis. In this way we can identify poorly integrated planets and energies that can impact success.

Parallel and Contra-Parallel Aspects

As well as relating by the principle Ptolemaic aspects we generally consider, planets also connect powerfully when they are in aspect by declination.

Aspects by declination are less obvious and apparent in the appearance of the chart, but can often 'explain' certain otherwise mysterious life experiences or tendencies.

Parallel aspects have the nature of conjunctions, contra-parallel that of oppositions. We only consider an orb of 1 degree maximum.

e.g., A parallel connection between Pluto and the Ascendant will explain why a native is strongly 'Plutonic' in their character and experiences, despite no major Scorpio placements or Pluto aspects on the chart.

Out of Bounds Planets

Examination of declinations of the planets will also show those planets which are 'out of bounds', where their eccentric orbits are at extremes and the declinations in excess of 23 degrees away from the ecliptic.

Out of bounds planets have a Uranian quality and express themselves in unique ways.

They are 'out of the sight of the King' and are extreme, rebellious, brave, eccentric, wild, rule breaking and generally out of the norm. They show areas where the native breaks boundaries and breaks away from situations. Out of bounds planets are frequently associated with zany and unusual characters, geniuses even, or more problematically with unacceptable behaviours or perhaps insanity.

The Moon, Mars, Mercury, Venus, Uranus and Pluto are planets most likely to travel out of bounds.

The Sun, Saturn, Neptune, Chiron and the lunar nodes do not go out of bounds.

If a career planet is out of bounds, or in aspect natally or by transit to an out of bounds planet, this will be significant to the vocational path.

People with an out of bounds Moon have a very strong and reliable intuition that they are likely to honour. They are independent individualists who march to their own drum. The lunar qualities of emotional intelligence, the ability to connect, inspire, attract and enthuse others are very apparent. They are liberated, spontaneous and emancipated people who can attract fame. They can show a high level of empathy, compassion and humanitarianism. A dark or negative expression would give alienation, lack of common politeness or sensitivity to others, rejection of all rules and restrictions and sociopathic or even criminal behaviour. Out of bounds Moon people can feel they don't fit in; are outsiders marching to a different drum and are possibly ahead of their time.

Mars out of bounds has been famously associated with violence and serial killers. However, that is to focus on the negative expression of Martian energies. It is possible for the conscious person to channel the out of bounds energies for good. Mars is about ambition, drive, desire, and bravery. It can indicate high physical energy levels. Tony Howard, who researches out-of-bounds planets, writes that it is more often associated with innovation, trendsetting and originality in art than violence (although OOB Mars people do tend to be feisty!). OOB Mars artists include Bjork and Frieda Kahlo and film maker David Lynch. Out of the box OOB Mars thinkers like Karl Marx and Martin Luther King influenced and changed society profoundly. It is about channelling the Martian energies in positive ways and consciously choosing the more evolved and higher expression, especially in the face of conflict.

Out of bounds Venus at its best shows a highly romantic nature, a popular person with charisma and magnetism beyond the norm. They can seduce, charm and entertain. They may be artistic or musical or have a keen eye for style and beauty. It is typical they have a strong appreciation for creature comforts and may be quite extravagant.

Cher is a good example of an out-of-bounds Venus person. She has won many plaudits for her acting skills, has had many musical hits as well as being a fashion designer, author and running a production company.

With Mercury out of bounds we see high innovative thought processes and high intelligence. These people have great communication skills, showing eloquence, charisma and the ability to strongly engage an audience. They can excel in fields such as literature, media, broadcasting, technology, engineering, science, medicine and mathematics.

With Uranus out of bounds we see very eccentric, unusual and zany personalities. They can be unique in appearance and behaviour, even having strange mannerisms and gestures. They have unbounded imagination and creativity and are associated with discovery, invention and experimentation. Freedom is sacred to them and they can be rebellious. An example of Uranus out of bounds is the painter Salvador Dali, famed for his surrealist images, bizarre films, photographs and sculpture as well as his unique appearance and unusual habits (like having an ocelot as a pet).

Pluto can also be out of bounds. It is already a planet of extremes. It also deals with deep, powerful issues (death, birth, transformation, evolution, transcendence) that are hard to quantify and although intense are frequently hidden, so it might be difficult to observe the impact on individuals. In some ways its impact is more generational than individual.

Pluto can be associated with organised crime, degeneration, the underworld, crime in general, terrorism, power and abuse, so one might look to see if these apply!

Planets going out of bounds by transit have effects on world events and finance and economics and must be explored.

Antiscia and Contra-Antiscia

The antiscia (plural of antiscion) or solstice point of a planet is a point opposite and equidistant across the solstitial divide. It is an ancient Hellenistic interpretation technique.

It is a shadow point, or a mirror, reflecting the darker side of a planet. It is a hidden point and can often illuminate an unexpected planetary expression.

It is worth checking if the antiscia point of a planet, especially, for our purposes, key career planets, are conjunct another planet: This is experienced like a conjunction to that planet. We might be surprised how a planetary energy seems to be expressed, but when we examine the antiscia point, we might find that it conjuncts another planet. We read this as a 'hidden conjunction' between the planet and the planet at the antiscia point. This operates within a close 1° orb. Perhaps someone Mercury in Gemini does not seem to have the easy flow of conversation and eager curiosity and lightness of expression we might anticipate; we might find for instance that the Mercury antiscia point is conjunct Saturn, so we see the sobering, restrictive impact of Saturn.

In vocational astrology we should check the antiscia for the ruler of the MC, planets in the 10th houses, the Sun and the Moon. This might reveal any blockages that might be affecting career success.

The contra-antiscia operates similarly, as a mirror point across the equinoctial axis, but is experienced like an opposition to the plant conjunct the contra-antiscia, again with a strict 1° orb.

Astrological software computes antiscia and contra-antiscia, but they can also be read form a simple chart like this:

ANTISCIA   CONTRA -ANTISCIA

Putting it All Together

In this book we have reviewed a number of techniques for working out all that the Midheaven of your chart has to tell you about achieving success in life.

You can systematically apply these techniques to your own birth chart, building an ever-clearer picture of your path to achievement.

The career path suggestions at every stage are not meant to be prescriptive, they are just examples of how the energy could be expressed. Blending all the energies you identify as you read through this book takes imagination and creativity. You will realise how, by applying a small number of techniques that are simple but powerful, you see infinite possibilities and how each of us has our own quite unique energetic fingerprint and unique self-expression to bring to the world.

- Firstly, consider the Midheaven and look first at the element and modality.
- Then find the Rising Sign and examine the element and modality there.
- Note the balance of elements, modes and polarities in your entire birth chart
- The fourth and seventh houses (the opposing angles) are going to show challenges to our personal expression.
- Note the house position of the Midheaven and the implications that describes.
- Consult the compendium of 38 Midheaven and Rising Sign combinations to see how these energies interact.
- Then find the ruler of the Midheaven and identify its house and sign position. These will give clues as to agreeable and potentially successful areas of work.
- Then look at any aspects to the Midheaven, by conjunction or other aspect. See the house ruler for those aspecting planets.

- Check if the 'suggestions' for all conditions of the Midheaven are in agreement with the Rising Sign. This where 'God's plan' for you confronts *your* plan for you (your free will). If there is no agreement, there is tweaking to be done and imagination to be applied in finding an expression that satisfies both imperatives.
- The Character of the Angles
- Check the modes of the angles:
  Mutable signs are about curiosity, change and busy-ness. This can make the person scattered. They may change jobs frequently. They get bored. The Fixed modality is about security and stability. They stick with things, like routine and can be stubborn. Cardinal signs an outlook of inspiration, challenge and driving ahead. They deal with the big issues.
- Check to see if the Ascendant/Descendant and Midheaven/IC are in harmony; also see if the angle modes relate to the personal planets. If they are jarringly different, for example a fixed Sun sign and mutable angles, this can be a difficult conflict of energies. An aspect between the rulers can indicate a path to resolution. Any aspect between angle rulers will be a key aspect for analysis. In this way we can identify poorly integrated planets and energies that can impact success.
- Then you can consider the Solar aspects and their information on your life mission to give another layer of nuance to your Midheaven picture.

Few things are as satisfying in life as finding work that is deeply fulfilling and expresses the true essence of who you are and uses your unique range of talents. If you have read this far, you have at your fingertips a comprehensive and easy to apply astrological 'toolbox' to identify your life path to success. Enjoy!

A Worksheet for Vocational Chart Analysis

FACTOR	DETAIL	INTERPRETATION	CAREER POSSIBILITIES
MC sign			
MC decan			
MC ruler sign			
MC ruler house			
Planets on MC			
Planets on Ascendant			
Planets on IC			
Planets on Descendant			
Elemental Balance			
Modal Balance			
Masculine/Feminine Balance			
Quadrant Emphasis			
Sun sign			
Sun house			
Sun decan			
Ascendant sign			
Ascendant decan			
Ascendant ruler			
Ascendant - MC correspondence			
Moon sign			

FACTOR	DETAIL	INTERPRETATION	CAREER POSSIBILITIES
Moon decan			
Moon house			
Natal Moon Phase			
Zenith			
Vertex			
Anti-vertex			
North Node house			
North Node sign			
IC blockages			
Moon blockages			
South node blockages			
Aspects to the MC			
Strongest Planet			
Saturn			
Saturn-Jupiter Phase			
Venus			
Day or Night Chart			
Part of Fortune			
Sedna			
Chiron			
Chiron Aspects			
Ceres			

FACTOR	DETAIL	INTERPRETATION	CAREER POSSIBILITIES
Vesta			
Hygeia			
Pallas Athena			
Parallel aspects			
Contra-parallel aspects			
Significant Antiscia aspects			
Significant Contra-Antiscia aspects